COMPREHENSION NINJA
INFERENCE AND BEYOND
LOWER KS2 FOR AGES 7–9

ANDREW JENNINGS

BLOOMSBURY EDUCATION
LONDON OXFORD NEW YORK NEW DELHI SYDNEY

BLOOMSBURY EDUCATION
Bloomsbury Publishing Plc
50 Bedford Square, London, WC1B 3DP, UK
Bloomsbury Publishing Ireland Limited
29 Earlsfort Terrace, Dublin 2, D02 AY28, Ireland

BLOOMSBURY, BLOOMSBURY EDUCATION and the Diana logo are trademarks of
Bloomsbury Publishing Plc

First published in Great Britain, 2025 by Bloomsbury Publishing Plc

Text copyright © Andrew Jennings, 2025

Illustrations copyright © Shutterstock

Andrew Jennings has asserted his right under the Copyright, Designs and Patents Act, 1988,
to be identified as Author of this work

All rights reserved. This publication may be photocopied solely for use in the educational establishment for which it was purchased, but may not be reproduced in any other form or by any other means – graphic, electronic, or mechanical, including photocopying, recording, taping or information storage or retrieval systems – without prior permission in writing from the publishers. No part of this publication may be used or reproduced in any way for the training, development or operation of artificial intelligence (AI) technologies, including generative AI technologies. The rights holders expressly reserve this publication from the text and data mining exception as per Article 4(3) of the Digital Single Market Directive (EU) 2019/790.

A catalogue record for this book is available from the British Library

ISBN: PB: 978-1-8019-9570-2; ePDF: 978-1-8019-9569-6

2 4 6 8 10 9 7 5 3 1

Text design by Marcus Duck Design

Printed and bound in India by Thomson Press (India) Ltd.

To find out more about our authors and books visit www.bloomsbury.com and
sign up for our newsletters

For product safety related questions contact: productsafety@bloomsbury.com

CONTENTS

INTRODUCTION 5

PART 1 8

1. Bella's Den...8
2. The Scots and the Picts 18
3. The Great Food Bank Heist 28
4. Stone Age Times 38
5. Ava's Gone and Pets in Class 48
6. Kid Normal 58
7. Wildsmith: Into the Dark Forest.........................68
8. The Journey of Ruby the Red Blood Cell 78

PART 2 88

9. Where I Live 88
10. The Voice of Vesuvius 92
11. Isadora Moon Sleepover 96
12. The Wild West 100
13. My Friend the Alien 104
14. The Jungle Personified 108
15. Mischief on the Moors 112
16. The Lab Notebook of Marie Curie 116
17. Mark of the Cyclops...120
18. The Boy Who Grew a Tree 124
19. Ping and the Missing Ring 128
20. Road Trip USA 132

ANSWERS 136

ACKNOWLEDGEMENTS 144

OTHER NINJA RESOURCES FOR TEACHERS

COMPREHENSION NINJA NON-FICTION

A set of six books for ages five to 11 that provide carefully curated resources to teach the key reading comprehension skills. With strong links to the National Curriculum, each book presents 24 high-quality non-fiction texts and photocopiable activities that help embed reading skills and improve comprehension, using strategies and question types such as true or false, labelling, matching, highlighting, filling in the gap, sequencing and multiple choice.

COMPREHENSION NINJA FICTION AND POETRY

Each book in this six-book set contains 24 immersive fiction extracts and poetry texts by acclaimed writers, including Roald Dahl, Michael Morpurgo, Patrice Lawrence, Katherine Rundell, David Almond, Zanib Mian, Joseph Coelho and Polly Ho-Yen. Every text is accompanied by photocopiable comprehension activities to boost reading retrieval skills in Key Stages 1 and 2.

NINJA MATHS RESOURCES

TIMES TABLES NINJA
SARAH FARRELL WITH ANDREW JENNINGS

The activities in these photocopiable books give Key Stage 1 and Key Stage 2 pupils all the tools they need to gain fluency in multiplication and division. The KS1 book focuses on the 2, 3, 4, 5 and 10 times tables, while the KS2 book covers the 2 to 12 times tables in detail, ready for the Year 4 multiplication tables check.

ARITHMETIC NINJA
ANDREW JENNINGS WITH SARAH FARRELL AND PAUL TUCKER

The Arithmetic Ninja series is the perfect resource for any primary classroom. Ideal for daily maths practice and quick lesson starters, each photocopiable book includes ten questions per day and 39 bonus weekly ninja challenges – 702 question cards in total.

FOR CHILDREN AT HOME AND IN THE CLASSROOM

WRITE LIKE A NINJA

A pocket-sized book packed full of all the grammar, vocabulary and sentence structures that children need in order to improve and develop their writing skills. Fully aligned to the Key Stage 2 National Curriculum, this book is designed to be used independently by pupils.

SPELL LIKE A NINJA

This book provides essential tips, lists and advice to support the teaching and learning of spelling in the classroom or at home. Including every statutory spelling pattern in the National Curriculum, this all-in-one quick reference tool enables pupils to learn at their own pace.

FURTHER RESOURCES FOR SCHOOLS, TEACHERS AND CHILDREN ONLINE

Head to www.vocabularyninja.co.uk and follow @VocabularyNinja on X (formerly Twitter) for more teaching and learning resources to support the teaching of vocabulary, reading, writing and the wider primary curriculum.

INTRODUCTION

COMPREHENSION NINJA: INFERENCE AND BEYOND

Inference is a natural skill that we use every day without really thinking about it. As we see, hear, experience things and interact with others we form opinions and make assumptions to draw logical conclusions. We might make inferences about how people are feeling, or why they did something based on small clues and behavioural indications that we have observed.

Inference is very similar in reading comprehension. The only difference is that we make assumptions and draw conclusions based on the descriptive words and language that we read, rather than through real life experiences. This is why everyday inference practice is so important. Speaking to people, playing and being around others help us to hone our skills and become more effective at making accurate inferences without even realising it. The good news is, that we can use our real-world inference skills to help us with inference in reading!

First, we need to understand the different comprehension inference question types and exactly what the questions are asking us to do. Then we can learn strategies for how to answer the questions to get those all-important marks. Comprehension Ninja Inference and Beyond will help to build confidence as pupils practice reading between the lines and searching for clues in the text. It contains a wealth of brilliant text extracts and thousands of questions to guide your pupils and embed inference learning.

- Simple questions
- Sentence inference
- This suggests
- Evidence
- Summarise
- Sequence
- Prediction

HOW INFERENCE LINKS TO SATS EXAM PRACTICE

At the end of Key Stage Two, children in Year 6 will complete a reading comprehension paper. This paper is made up of around 38-40 questions with 50 marks available. It's important to understand the format of these questions and the vital role that inference skills play in completing the test successfully. On average 40% of the marks available in the reading test are retrieval-style questions, which involves finding and presenting information from the text. Very straightforward and nearly half the marks in the test. The next 30-35% of the available marks are dedicated to inference-style questions, which are slightly more complex as they refer to information that isn't explicitly stated, but instead implied. If we can master both retrieval and inference, on average we have 75% of the SATs test questions tackled! So how do we start the journey of inference mastery?

Comprehension Ninja: Inference and Beyond is carefully structured and designed to mimic the appearance of inference questions in the Key Stage 2 SATs reading paper. This provides teachers, parents and pupils with the most comprehensive and realistic library of inference style questions, that will enable pupils to experience and improve their inference skills like never before.

HOW TO USE THIS BOOK

This book is extremely versatile and can be used in many ways. Here's a few ideas on ways you could use the texts and questions across KS2 to master inference and beyond.

BOOK BREAKDOWN

The book is split into two halves. The first 8 texts are for in depth inference practice. The extracts are followed by multiple pages of different question types, great for practicing specific skills. For example, you might wish to focus specifically on 3-mark impression questions over the course of a week or fortnight with the aim of improving that skill. You could look at a different text each day, alongside the corresponding 3-mark questions. Then the next week or fortnight you might focus on a different skill, such as 'summarising'. The children would encounter a familiar text, but the sets of questions would approach the text from different angles and strengthen different comprehension skills. This is a great way to embed inference into your daily, weekly or fortnightly reading routine.

The second half of the book has 12 texts, with shorter, double page sets of questions, that cover all the different question types. These texts and questions are better suited for interventions and ongoing assessments (both formative and summative). They are great for exposing children to all of the question types. You can set a time limit of 15-20 minutes to read and complete the questions to help pupils build the stamina and tempo needed for reading comprehension.

Whole Class Teaching: Use texts and specific question sets to model specific skills within your whole class or guided reading sessions.

Small Group Intervention: Use the front eight or back twelve texts to deliver small group interventions to dive into specific skills, or to assess how competent pupils are with specific question types.

Ongoing Assessment: The back twelve texts can be used to identify gaps in inference, as all inference style questions are covered, allowing for future follow-up lessons that focus on one particular inference skill.

Homework: Simple and easy to photocopy and provide pupils with regular homework activities.

Teacher or Teaching Assistant: The comprehensive nature of the books allows for all members of staff to dip in, access a high-quality text and thousands of questions. Perfect for saving time, while improving pupil performance outcomes.

THE TEXT EXTRACTS

Comprehension Ninja Inference and Beyond contains several different text types that children come across in Key Stage 2 literacy:

Non-Fiction: These informative texts focus on areas across the National Curriculum, but they also introduce historical figures or events that might not have been studied before. This is often the case in KS2 SATs, where non-fiction texts cover both curriculum topics and other more random subjects.

Historical Fiction: We have created some unique texts that blend curriculum subjects but are delivered from different perspectives. Using real world events such as the eruption of Mount Vesuvius, we have presented fictional characters or perspectives to explore the subject area. These texts are highly engaging fiction and are good springboards for classroom discussion surrounding non-fiction subject areas!

Fiction: We have curated a number of texts with provoking characters, diverse environments and stimulating situations written by well-known children's authors. The aim is to provide texts that are similar in complexity and style to the types of fiction in the KS2 SATs papers.

Poetry: We have included a blend of light-hearted poetry as well as more serious, reflective poems to both entertain pupils and encourage them to 'read between the lines'. Our poets and their extracts are some of the most well-known and celebrated in the literary world.

THE QUESTION TYPES

SIMPLE QUESTIONS

Super straightforward 'how' and 'why' questions direct pupils to specific parts of the text and guide them to make inferences and explain the reasoning behind their answers. Pupils might be asked: 'How do you know?' or 'Why did this happen…?'. These questions offer one mark.

> **NINJA NOTES**
> These questions relate to the actions or emotions of the characters in the text. Sometimes these questions only require one word or a short phrase to answer.

SENTENCE INFERENCE

Sentence inference questions provide an opportunity for pupils to zone in on a specific sentence or word in the text to draw a conclusion. These questions are presented in a variety of styles with pupils asked to either tick boxes or write down their inference in a short sentence. These questions offer one mark.

> **NINJA NOTES**
> When it comes to 'tick the box' questions, ensure that pupils are not just guessing. It's important for pupils to read the questions and make a logical inference based on the information provided. Pupils should focus on the actions and emotions and try to draw on their own experiences to imagine how characters in the text might feel, act or think.

THIS SUGGESTS

This suggests questions are presented in a multiple-choice format. A sentence or short extract is provided, with an inference that needs to be drawn and a few suggested answers. Pupils need to decide on and tick the most logical option. These questions offer one mark.

> **NINJA NOTES**
> These questions often refer to the imagery and language that authors use to create an atmosphere, such as simile, metaphor and personification describing the actions or emotions of a character. Check that pupils understand that 'this suggests' simply means 'this shows that' or 'this means'.

EVIDENCE: TWO MARKS – TWO INFERENCES

These questions direct pupils to specific parts of the text, where they will need to re-read sentences or even a paragraph. The pupil then needs to answer a question and give two ways that something is inferred or presumed. Pupils need to look for clues in the text and provide two pieces of evidence that show or support what the question is asking. Each piece of evidence is worth one mark, with two marks available in total.

> **NINJA NOTES**
> These questions require pupils to look for evidence that supports an inference. The question might ask: 'How can you tell the child was upset? Give two ways'. Pupils need to reflect on their own understanding of what an upset child looks like and then look for clues that suggest this in the text. For example, there may be inferences such as 'they were crying' and 'they couldn't catch their breath'. Both these inferences are worth one mark each. Pupils don't need to write expansive answers that are complete sentences; they just need to provide the evidence.

🔍 EVIDENCE: THREE MARKS – THREE INFERENCES

Three-mark evidence questions are very common and straightforward too. Much like the two-mark questions, these questions require pupils to provide three pieces of evidence that support an inference, or to provide three inferences. These questions normally have two lines available for each piece of evidence to be written. These questions often refer to the whole text, meaning the answers can be drawn from anywhere across the whole text, not just a specific paragraph.

> **NINJA NOTES**
>
> Teach pupils to read the question carefully and the instructions that are provided. If the question references the 'whole text' then pupils must know that the inferences or the evidence could be found anywhere across the text. Alternatively, if they are directed to a specific part of the text, they will need to focus in on that area of the text.

🔍 EVIDENCE: THREE MARKS – IMPRESSION AND EVIDENCE

Impression and evidence questions require pupils to do multiple tasks for three marks. The question is laid out so that pupils need to provide inferences or impressions and look for supporting evidence. Pupils might be directed to specific areas of the text or to the whole text. An 'impression' is essentially the reader's opinion or what they think, so the answers should be written in the pupil's own words.

> **NINJA NOTES**
>
> Expose pupils to these questions early on. They are actually fairly simple and should not be feared. Teach pupils to provide a simple impression or opinion. Quite often, the impression box will be a one-word description, such as happy, anxious, excited, old, etc. In the evidence box, pupils just need to provide evidence from the text to support their impression. For example, if their impression was 'it's old' the evidence in the text might be, 'the walls were crumbling.' That's it. No need for complete, explanatory sentences. What impression is really asking is, what do you think or how does this make you feel?

💭 SUMMARISE QUESTIONS

Summarise questions are multiple choice and give an opportunity for pupils to demonstrate that they understand the main idea of the text. Pupils are presented with a selection of statements and are required to select the one that best matches or reflects the events, feelings and atmosphere presented in the text. These questions offer one mark.

> Summarise questions not only focus on the events that happened in the text, but they also summarise character and narrator attitudes, feelings, emotions and thoughts. This involves reflecting carefully on the general emotions, thoughts, actions or tone of the characters or narrators and selecting the statement that matches. In lessons, prompt pupils to explain and discuss why they chose a particular option, to avoid pupils just randomly choosing an answer.

123 SEQUENCE QUESTIONS

These questions require pupils to sequence information in the order it occurs in the text, from first to last.

💭 PREDICTION QUESTIONS

Prediction questions ask the pupil to think beyond the text and choose the statement that best matches what could happen next. These require pupils to think about what has been implied in the text already to then make a logical prediction or guess about the future. These are multiple choice style questions, offering one mark.

> **NINJA NOTES**
>
> Prediction questions encourage pupils to reflect on details stated in the text, but they also rely on our understanding of the world and our previous experiences to help us make logical or sensible predictions.

BELLA'S DEN

BERLIE DOHERTY

From *Bella's Den* by Berlie Doherty © Berlie Doherty, 1997, published by Barrington Stoke, reproduced by kind permission of David Higham Associates.

The Middle of the World

Bella has a secret – one that she is very good at keeping. That secret is a den hidden on a little muddy hill, wild amid the trees and nestled beside some foxes with a den of their own.

We must have been in the den for almost an hour. There wasn't room for both of us to lie down, so we sat crouched together with Bella's sleeping bag pulled across us both.

We were both staring out into the night. It was so dark that it was like a black curtain, just too far away to reach out and touch.

Then the moon slid away from the clouds and shone over the grass that covered the den. All of a sudden it was as bright as day. And I think I was the first to see it.

I was looking at the big mound below the den. I was thinking how the moon made it look like a stage with the lights on, and how deep and black those holes were, when I saw something move.

I touched Bella's arm and she let out a little breath of, yes, I've seen it too.

It was a fox.

He grew out of the darkness of the hole, and then took shape as the moon lit him. He stood as if he had been turned to stone, and he was looking right at our den, right past the grassy strands, right at me.

It was as if he was locked into me, reading my mind. I didn't dare move or breathe. I didn't dare do anything but look back at him, till my eyes blurred. I was holding myself so still that I thought I would pass out. My skin was ice cold, frozen cold with fear.

From *Bella's Den* by Berlie Doherty © Berlie Doherty, 1997, published by Barrington Stoke, reproduced by kind permission of David Higham Associates.

1

FICTION

Then all of a sudden, the fox seemed to relax. He turned his head just a little, and, as if it was a signal, out came another fox and three little cubs. Four shapes loomed out of the hole, each one faster than the one before. They were jumping out like little kids in a school playground, tumbling red and brown and silvery white.

The dog fox slunk off into the shadows.

The other big fox, his vixen, sat just where he had been, at the front of the hole. She pricked up her ears and her head turned from time to time as she listened out for all kinds of sounds in the hills.

But the three cubs had come out to play. They biffed each other and fell over and rolled about. They jumped on each other, jumped on the vixen, hid from each other and played roly-poly right down to the river.

I could hear them breathing, and scuffling with their paws. I could hear the little puffs of sound they made when they biffed each other.

It felt as if this little patch of ground where the foxes were playing was the middle of the world. It felt as if nothing else that was happening anywhere was as important as this.

I've no idea what the signal was but, quick as a flash, the vixen turned her head, sharp. The cubs scrambled up the bank and one by one slid back into the hole. The vixen waited a moment, lifted her head then melted down into the hole after them. She slid into it like water.

It went dark again, as if the moon had been put out.

I'm not sure if I really saw it or not, but then I think I saw another shape, like a dark flutter where the hole was, and a dull white glow like the tip of a tail vanishing into it.

1 BELLA'S DEN

✏ SIMPLE QUESTIONS

Look at the paragraph beginning...

1. 'We must have been in the den for almost an hour.'
   How can you tell that the den is small?

   _____

2. 'Then the moon slid away from the clouds.'
   Why do you think the moonlight surprised them?

   _____

3. 'I was looking at the big mound below the den.'
   How can you tell that the hole looked mysterious?

   _____

4. 'He grew out of the darkness of the hole...'
   Why do you think the fox stood still?

   _____

5. 'It was as if he was locked into me...'
   How can you tell the narrator was frightened?

   _____

6 'Then all of a sudden the fox seemed to relax.'
Why do you think the other foxes appeared after the first fox relaxed?

_____

7 'But the three cubs had come out to play.'
How can you tell that the cubs were playful?

_____

8 'It felt as if this little patch of ground…'
Why do you think the narrator felt the foxes were in the 'middle of the world'?

_____

9 'I've no idea what the signal was but…'
How can you tell the vixen was alert to danger?

_____

10 'I'm not sure if I really saw it or not…'
Why do you think the narrator felt unsure about what they saw at the end?

_____

1 BELLA'S DEN

SENTENCE INFERENCE

1 'I touched Bella's arm and she let out a little breath of, yes, I've seen it too.'
How can you tell that the narrator and Bella are trying to be quiet?

_____

2 'It felt as if this little patch of ground where the foxes were playing was the middle of the world.' What are Bella and the narrator feeling in this moment?
A sense of… Tick **one**.

- happiness ☐
- wonder ☐
- tiredness ☐
- excited ☐

3 'The cubs scrambled up the bank and one by one slid back into the hole.'
What does the word **'scrambled'** tell you about how the cubs moved?

_____

4 'He stood as if he had been turned to stone, and he was looking right at our den, right past the grassy strands, right at me.'
How would you describe the fox's state of mind at this point? Tick **one**.

- curious ☐
- tired ☐
- wary ☐
- sad ☐

5 'I could hear them breathing, and scuffling with their paws. I could hear the little puffs of sound they made when they biffed each other.'
What do you think is happening when the narrator says **'they biffed each other'**?

_____

1 BELLA'S DEN

💭 THIS SUGGESTS...

1 'It was as if he was locked into me, reading my mind. I didn't dare move or breathe.'
What does this suggest about how the narrator feels when the fox looks at them?

The narrator feels calm. ☐

The narrator feels scared. ☐

The narrator feels happy. ☐

2 'Then all of a sudden the fox seemed to relax. He turned his head just a little, and, as if it was a signal, out came another fox and three little cubs.'
What does this suggest about the fox's behaviour?

The fox feels playful. ☐

The fox feels aggressive. ☐

The fox feels safe. ☐

3 'It felt as if this little patch of ground where the foxes were playing was the middle of the world.'
What does this suggest about how the narrator views the foxes' playtime?

It feels magical and special. ☐

It feels boring. ☐

It feels scary. ☐

4 'She slid into it like water.'
What does this suggest about how the vixen enters the den?

She moves quickly and smoothly. ☐

She moves clumsily. ☐

She moves very slowly. ☐

1 BELLA'S DEN

EVIDENCE – TWO MARKS

Look at the paragraph beginning...

1 'It was as if he was locked into me, reading my mind.' How can you tell that the narrator feels frightened when the fox looks at them? Give **two** ways.

1 _____

2 _____

2 'Then all of a sudden...' How can you tell that the fox feels safe when the cubs come out to play? Give **two** ways.

1 _____

2 _____

3 'They biffed each other and fell over and rolled about.' How can you tell that the cubs are enjoying themselves? Give **two** ways.

1 _____

2 _____

4 'It went dark again, as if the moon had been put out.' How can you tell that the narrator feels unsure about what they saw at the end? Give **two** ways.

1 _____

2 _____

1 BELLA'S DEN

🔍 EVIDENCE – THREE MARKS

1 Look at the whole text. How can you tell that the narrator feels amazed by the foxes' behaviour? Give **three** ways.

1 _____
_____
_____

2 _____
_____
_____

3 _____
_____
_____

1 BELLA'S DEN

🔍 EVIDENCE – THREE MARKS

2 What impression do you get of the narrator's feelings about the night? Give **two** impressions, using evidence from the text to support your answer.

Impression	Evidence

3 What impression do you get of the fox cubs? Give **two** impressions, using evidence from the text to support your answer.

Impression	Evidence

1 BELLA'S DEN

🔮 SUMMARY AND PREDICTION

SUMMARISE

1 What statement best describes Bella's attitude toward the den? Tick **one**.

Bella sees it as a secret and special place. ☐

Bella doesn't care much about the den. ☐

Bella finds the den uncomfortable and scary. ☐

2 What statement best describes the narrator's feelings after seeing the vixen and cubs vanish? Tick **one**.

The narrator feels confused about what they saw. ☐

The narrator feels awe at the magical moment. ☐

The narrator feels frightened by the darkness. ☐

SEQUENCE

3 Number the following sentences from 1–4 to show the order they happen in the text. The first one has been done for you.

Awe and wonder at the magical moment. ☐

Excitement at seeing something move. ☐ 1

Fear as the fox stares directly at the narrator. ☐

Confusion as the den returns to darkness. ☐

PREDICTION

4 What do you think might happen next after the foxes disappear into the den?

The narrator will try to explore the foxes' den. ☐

Bella and the narrator will decide to visit the den again another night. ☐

They will never see the foxes again. ☐

THE SCOTS AND THE PICTS

ANDREW JENNINGS

The Middle of the World

Long ago, Scotland was home to ancient tribes with rich cultures. Two of the most famous were the Scots and the Picts, who shaped the history of Scotland with their battles, migrations and alliances.

The Scots: Warriors from Ireland

The Scots didn't originally come from Scotland – they came from Ireland. In the early centuries, a tribe called the Scotti sailed across the sea to western Scotland and settled in a region on the coast known as Dal Riata. These skilled warriors and sailors brought their language, Gaelic, and a rich culture with them.

The Scots quickly became powerful, establishing kingdoms and making alliances with other tribes. Over time, they expanded their influence, mingling with local peoples and leaving a lasting mark on Scotland's history.

The Picts: The Painted People

The Picts lived in Scotland long before the Scots arrived. Known as the 'painted ones' because they tattooed or painted their bodies with intricate designs, they were fierce warriors who lived in northern and eastern Scotland.

The Picts built strong hillforts to defend their land from invaders like the Romans, who found them difficult to conquer. While the Picts didn't leave behind many written records, their artwork, especially the Pictish stones – decorated with symbols of animals and people – remain a testament to their culture.

Clashing and Uniting

The Scots and the Picts were often in conflict, battling for land and power. The Picts were determined to defend their territories, while the Scots sought to expand. However, both groups faced a greater threat – the Vikings, who began raiding Scotland's coasts.

To face the Viking menace, the Scots and Picts eventually united. In the 9th century, Kenneth MacAlpin, a king of the Scots, is believed to have become king of the Picts as well. This union marked the beginning of the Kingdom of Scotland, combining the strengths of both tribes.

Life in Ancient Scotland

Life for the Scots and Picts wasn't easy. They lived in small villages, farming and raising animals. Both tribes had rich spiritual traditions, worshipping gods connected to nature. They also valued sacred sites like stone circles and wells.

The Scots, with their roots in Ireland, introduced Christianity to Scotland. Monks from Ireland, and later from other parts of Europe, built monasteries, spreading the new faith. The island of Iona, founded by Scottish monks, became an important religious and learning centre.

The Legacy of the Scots and Picts

The union of the Scots and Picts helped create the foundations of modern Scotland. The Scots' language, Gaelic, became widespread, and the influence of Christianity spread throughout the land. Meanwhile, the Picts left behind their stone carvings and proud stories of fierce independence.

Traces of the Scots and Picts live on today in the names of places, ancient forts and Scotland's cultural identity.

2 THE SCOTS AND THE PICTS

SIMPLE QUESTIONS

Look at the paragraph beginning...

1 'The Scots didn't originally come from Scotland.'
Why do you think the Scots decided to settle in Dal Riata?

_____

2 'The Picts lived in Scotland...'
Why do you think they were called the 'painted ones'?

_____

3 'The Scots quickly became powerful...'
How can you tell that the Scots were skilled warriors?

_____

4 'The Picts built...'
Why do you think the Romans had a hard time conquering the Picts?

_____

5 'To face the Viking menace...'
Why did the Scots and Picts decide to unite?

_____

6 'To face the Viking menace...'
Why do you think his rule was important for Scotland?

_____

7 'Life for the Scots and Picts wasn't easy...'
How can you tell that the Scots and Picts valued the outdoors?

_____

8 'The Scots, with their roots in Ireland...'
How can you tell that monks were important in spreading the new religion?

_____

9 'The union of the Scots and Picts...'
How can you tell that the Picts wanted to share their history?

_____

10 'The union of the Scots and Picts...'
Why do you think the Scots and Picts are still important to Scotland?

_____

2 THE SCOTS AND THE PICTS

SENTENCE INFERENCE

1 'The island of Iona, founded by Scottish monks, became an important religious and learning centre.' What does the word **'island'** tell you that the island is surrounded by?

_____

2 'The Scots quickly became powerful, establishing kingdoms and making alliances with other tribes.' What does this sentence tell you about the relationship between tribes? They… Tick **one**.

- fought ☐
- worked together ☐
- hated each other ☐
- ignored each other ☐

3 'The Scots, with their roots in Ireland, introduced Christianity to Scotland.' What does the word **'roots'** tell us about where the Scots came from?

_____

4 'Both tribes had rich spiritual traditions, worshipping gods connected to nature. They also valued sacred sites like stone circles and wells.'

What does this passage tell you that both tribes had? A strong sense of… Tick **one**.

- wellbeing ☐
- warfare ☐
- family ☐
- religion ☐

5 'To face the Viking menace, the Scots and Picts eventually united.'

What does this sentence tell you about what the Scots and Picts did to fight the Vikings?

_____

2 THE SCOTS AND THE PICTS

💭 THIS SUGGESTS...

1 'The Scots quickly became powerful, establishing kingdoms and making alliances with other tribes.'
What does this suggest about the Scots' influence in ancient Scotland?

- [ ] The Scots were weak and unimportant.
- [ ] The Scots had a lot of influence.
- [ ] The Scots were only interested in farming.

2 'The Picts built strong hillforts to defend their land from invaders like the Romans.'
What does this suggest about the Picts' attitude towards their land?

- [ ] The Picts valued and wanted to protect their land.
- [ ] The Picts were eager to leave their land.
- [ ] The Picts wanted to share their land with everyone.

3 'To face the Viking menace, the Scots and Picts eventually united.'
What does this suggest about the relationship between the Scots and Picts during the Viking attacks?

- [ ] They remained enemies.
- [ ] They realised they were stronger together.
- [ ] They tried to ignore the Vikings.

4 'Known as the 'painted ones' because they tattooed or painted their bodies with intricate designs.'
What does this suggest about Pictish culture?

- [ ] They didn't care about appearance.
- [ ] They only cared about fighting.
- [ ] They had unique and artistic traditions.

2 THE SCOTS AND THE PICTS

🔍 EVIDENCE – TWO MARKS

Look at the paragraph beginning...

1. 'The Scots didn't originally come from Scotland…'
   How can you tell that the Scots were adventurous? Give **two** ways.

   1 _____

   2 _____

2. 'Known as the 'painted ones'…'
   How can you tell that the Picts were proud of their appearance? Give **two** ways.

   1 _____

   2 _____

3. 'The Scots and Picts…'
   How can you tell that the Picts were protective of their land? Give **two** ways.

   1 _____

   2 _____

4. 'The Scots and Picts…'
   How can you tell that life was challenging for the Scots and Picts? Give **two** ways.

   1 _____

   2 _____

2 THE SCOTS AND THE PICTS

🔍 EVIDENCE – THREE MARKS

1 Look at the whole text. Give **three** pieces of evidence that show the Scots were determined to make an impact in Scotland.

1 _____

_____

_____

2 _____

_____

_____

3 _____

_____

_____

2 THE SCOTS AND THE PICTS

🔍 EVIDENCE – THREE MARKS

2 What impression do you get of the Picts' attitude towards their land?
Give **two** impressions using evidence from the text to support your impressions.

Impression	Evidence

3 What impression do you get of the Scots' approach to settling in Scotland?
Give **two** impressions using evidence from the text to support your impressions.

Impression	Evidence

2 THE SCOTS AND THE PICTS
SUMMARY AND PREDICTION

SUMMARISE

1 How did the relationship between the Scots and Picts change after the Viking invasions? Tick **one**.

They kept fighting each other. ☐

They joined together to fight the Vikings. ☐

The Scots took over the Picts' land. ☐

2 What statement best describes the journey and fate of the Picts over time? Tick **one**.

The Picts became rulers of Scotland. ☐

The Picts left Scotland to escape threats. ☐

The Picts stayed strong but later joined with the Scots. ☐

SEQUENCE

3 Number the following sentences from 1–4 to show the order they happen in the text. The first one has been done for you.

Kenneth MacAlpin united the Scots and Picts into one kingdom. ☐

The Picts built strong hillforts to defend their land. ☐

The Vikings began raiding the coasts of Scotland. ☐

The Scots sailed from Ireland to settle in Dal Riata. [1]

PREDICTION

4 If the Scots and Picts hadn't united against the Vikings, what might have happened? Tick **one**.

The Scots and Picts would have defeated the Vikings separately. ☐

The Scots and Picts might have focused on farming instead of fighting. ☐

The Vikings might have taken over more land in Scotland. ☐

THE GREAT FOOD BANK HEIST

ONJALI Q. RAÚF

The Real Hunger Games

I hated the months when we had to be little troopers. They were always hard because the games we played at home suddenly didn't feel like fun anymore. Nothing was ever fun when you were so hungry you felt as if you were full of gaps and holes.

Normally the games we played made everything feel ten thousand per cent better. And that was all because of Mum. She became a games inventor when dad left us and she had to go to the food bank for the first time. She came home with some things we liked and lots we didn't like at all. So to stop me and Ashley feeling as if we didn't want to eat the meal she made, Mum came up with all sorts of games.

My favourite one had to be Master Chef, which was when I got to choose all of the weirdest ingredients the food bank had given us and cook a meal out of them. Mum's friend from the hospital had even given me a real chef's hat with a real burnt hole in it to wear when I was playing it!

So far I'd come up with gherkin hotdogs, tuna and jam pie, and noodles swirled with mustard and brown sauce. But the dish I was most famous for was Pineapple Surprise, which was bread soaked in lemonade and fried, topped with large, round pineapple slices from a tin and put in the oven so that it looked like a burger. I had never seen Mum's face look so funny as when she was eating that one!

The game Ashley loved best was the Menu Makers Game. We played that after every visit to the bank. We made a list of everything the food bank had given us and then invented a proper menu – just like you get in a restaurant.

Ashley loved drawing and colouring in, so her menus were always the prettiest. When she did an extra special one, Mum stuck it on the fridge. My favourite menu Ashley made was covered with pictures of mushrooms with salad leaves as wings, and fish with lots of fingers.

From *The Great (Food) Bank Heist*, reprinted by permission of HarperCollins Publishers Ltd © 2021, Onjali Q. Raúf

3

FICTION

But there was one game we didn't really enjoy at all. Even Mum didn't like it, although she pretended she did. It was called the Transformers Game. We always played that in a Little Troopers Month, and sometimes we had to play it a few times.

It was where you looked at food that you didn't want to eat – not even a little bit! – and used your imagination to make it something extra tasty and delicious, and then told everyone about it. Mum said she had invented it to help our imaginations grow stronger.

It was hard, but sometimes it did work. One time I transformed a horrible, lumpy, bright red sandwich filled with nothing but extra-squashy wet tomatoes into a huge roast chicken with a mountain of mashed potatoes with lots of butter melting down it like a volcano. I didn't have those things, but imagining them made me not mind eating the sandwich so much.

But in a Little Troopers Month, playing any of those games felt like hard work.

It was hard trying to make a menu when you didn't have much food to write out on it. And it was hard being a Master Chef when there weren't enough ingredients, no matter how nice and burnt-looking the hole in your chef's hat was. And it was especially hard when you had spent a whole day thinking about food – even in the middle of playing football or reading a book or trying to figure out your nine times table – and made yourself tired. At times like that your imagination sometimes didn't want to transform something horrible into something better.

And sometimes none of the games worked at all, and everyone was just acting and pretending that they weren't hungry when really they were so hungry that they couldn't sleep at night and cried when they thought no one else could hear them… Even Mum… Especially Mum.

3 THE GREAT FOOD BANK HEIST

SIMPLE QUESTIONS

Look at the paragraph beginning...

1 'I hated the months when we had to be little troopers.'
How can you tell that Little Troopers Months were difficult?

_____

2 'Normally the games we played made everything feel ten thousand per cent better.' Why do you think the games made things better for the narrator and Ashley?

_____

3 'My favourite one had to be...'
Why do you think the narrator enjoyed the Master Chef game?

_____

4 'Mum's friend from the hospital had even given me a real chef's hat.'
Why do you think the narrator was proud of the chef's hat?

_____

5 'The game Ashley loved best was the Menu Makers Game.'
How can you tell that Ashley puts the most work into creating the menus?

_____

6 'But there was one game we didn't really enjoy at all.'
Why do you think the family didn't like the Transformers Game?

_____

7 'It was where you looked at food...'
Why do you think Mum wanted them to play the Transformers Game?

_____

8 'It was hard trying to make a menu when you didn't have much food.'
How can you tell that Little Troopers Months were tough for the narrator?

_____

9 'It was hard trying to make a menu when you didn't have much food.'
How can you tell that hunger affected their games?

_____

10 'And sometimes none of the games worked at all.'
How can you tell that Mum was also struggling during Little Troopers Months?

_____

3 THE GREAT FOOD BANK HEIST
SENTENCE INFERENCE

1. 'But the dish I was most famous for was Pineapple Surprise…'
   Why do you think Mum's face looked so funny eating this dish?
   _____

2. 'So far I'd come up with gherkin hotdogs, tuna and jam pie, and noodles swirled with mustard and brown sauce. But the dish I was most famous for was Pineapple Surprise…'
   How does the narrator feel as they describe their recipes? A sense of…
   Tick **one**.

   frustration ☐
   pride ☐
   excitement ☐
   hunger ☐

3. '…a huge roast chicken with a mountain of mashed potatoes with lots of butter melting down it like a volcano.'
   What does the phrase **'like a volcano'** tell you about the butter?
   _____

4. '…when really they were so hungry that they couldn't sleep at night and cried when they thought no one else could hear them…Even Mum…Especially Mum.'
   How is Mum feeling when everyone is beyond hungry? Tick **one**.

   uninterested ☐
   helpless ☐
   creative ☐
   careless ☐

5. 'But in a Little Troopers Month, playing any of those games felt like hard work.'
   How does the narrator feel about Little Troopers Months?
   _____

3 THE GREAT FOOD BANK HEIST

💭 THIS SUGGESTS...

1 'Mum came up with all sorts of games.'
What does this suggest about Mum's attitude towards the difficult times?

   She is strict. ☐

   She is creative. ☐

   She is careless. ☐

2 'My favourite one had to be Master Chef, which was when I got to choose all of the weirdest ingredients the food bank had given us and cook a meal out of them.'
What does this suggest about how the narrator feels about cooking?

   They find it boring. ☐

   They find it fun. ☐

   They find it frustrating. ☐

3 'Ashley loved drawing and colouring in, so her menus were always the prettiest.'
What does this suggest about Ashley's personality?

   She is serious. ☐

   She is lazy. ☐

   She is creative. ☐

4 'And sometimes none of the games worked at all, and everyone was just acting and pretending that they weren't hungry.'
What does this suggest about the family's situation during Little Troopers Months?

   They are relaxed. ☐

   They are struggling. ☐

   They are comfortable. ☐

3 THE GREAT FOOD BANK HEIST

🔍 EVIDENCE – TWO MARKS

Look at the paragraph beginning…

1. 'Normally the games we played made everything feel ten thousand per cent better.' How can you tell that Mum tried to make the food bank food enjoyable for her children? Give **two** ways.

    1 _____

    2 _____

2. 'My favourite one had to be Master Chef.' How can you tell that the narrator finds the Master Chef game interesting? Give **two** ways.

    1 _____

    2 _____

3. How can you tell that Ashley enjoyed making the menus? Give **two** ways.

    1 _____

    2 _____

5. 'And sometimes none of the games worked at all.' How can you tell that Little Troopers Months were especially hard for the family? Give **two** ways.

    1 _____

    2 _____

3 THE GREAT FOOD BANK HEIST

🔍 EVIDENCE – THREE MARKS

1. Look at the whole text. How can you tell that Mum was determined to keep her children happy despite their struggles?

   1 _____

   2 _____

   3 _____

3 THE GREAT FOOD BANK HEIST

🔍 EVIDENCE – THREE MARKS

2 What impression do you get of Mum's attitude towards her children during hard times? Give **two** impressions, using evidence from the text to support your answer.

Impression	Evidence

3 What impression do you get of the narrator's feelings about the games? Give **two** impressions, using evidence from the text to support your answer.

Impression	Evidence

③ THE GREAT FOOD BANK HEIST

🔮 SUMMARY AND PREDICTION

SUMMARISE

1 What best describes the narrator's feelings about Mum during the story?

- He feels annoyed that Mum makes them play games. ☐
- He admires Mum for trying to make things better for them. ☐
- He thinks Mum enjoys Little Troopers Months. ☐

2 What best describes Mum's approach to dealing with difficult times?

- Mum stays positive by creating games to make meals more enjoyable. ☐
- Mum doesn't like talking about hard times and avoids them. ☐
- Mum relies on her children to solve the family's problems. ☐

SEQUENCE

3 Number the following sentences from 1–4 to show the order they happen in the text. The first one has been done for you.

- He feels proud when playing the Master Chef game. ☐
- He feels frustrated during Little Troopers Months. ☐
- He feels sad when they hear Mum crying at night. ☐
- He feels hungry but uses his imagination to cope. [1]

PREDICTION

4 How might the narrator reset if he has to play the Transformers Game again?

- He will refuse to play the game because it's too hard. ☐
- He will imagine his least favourite food as something amazing. ☐
- He will make Ashley play the game instead. ☐

THE STONE AGE TIMES

Breaking News:
Fire Discovered by Local Genius

By Flint Rockwell, Reporter

In what can only be described as the hottest discovery of the Stone Age, local hunter-gatherer, Thag Flintfoot, has changed the course of history by inventing fire. This ground-breaking discovery has sent shockwaves through the Stone Age community, and life may never be the same again.

The Discovery

According to Thag, the momentous event happened entirely by accident while he was trying to break open some rocks. 'I was just banging two stones together, like usual,' he explained, still smelling faintly of smoke. 'Then – whoosh! – there was a spark, and next thing I knew, the dry grass in front of me was on fire!'

Thag, whose greatest life accomplishment was successfully herding mammoths away from his camp, quickly realised that this strange, glowing phenomenon could be useful. 'At first, I thought I'd angered the gods or something,' he admitted. 'But then I noticed that the fire was warm. And that was a real game-changer.'

Fire: What Does It Mean for Us?

The implications of Thag's discovery are enormous. For one thing, it seems like mealtimes will never be the same again. Until now, Stone Age humans have relied on raw meat and berries, with many complaining about how difficult it is to chew mammoth steak without breaking a tooth. With fire, they can now cook their meals, making food more tender and, according to Thag, 'much tastier'.

'I threw some meat on the flames, and it came out all crispy on the outside but soft in the middle,' Thag told us. 'No more gnawing for hours on raw meat – this will really change how we live.'

But the benefits don't stop at the dinner table. Fire can also be used for warmth,

FICTIONAL NEWSPAPER ARTICLE

keeping people cosy during cold nights without needing to pile on extra mammoth furs. It also seems to scare away wild animals. 'I had some wolves circling the camp last night, but when they saw the fire, they ran off,' Thag said proudly. 'I think they're afraid of it.'

Expert Reactions: What Others Are Saying

Thag's fellow tribespeople are still wrapping their heads around the discovery, though reactions have been mixed. Oog Gruntsson, a neighbour, expressed excitement about the potential for easier living. 'Fire warm, fire good,' he said.
'Me tired of cold nights and raw food.'

However, not everyone is so sure. Bora Rocksmash, a respected elder of the tribe, is a bit sceptical. 'I'm all for the warmth,' she said, 'but we need to be careful. Fire dangerous. Thag already burned hole in his own loincloth.'

What's Next for Thag?

When asked about his future plans, Thag looked thoughtful for a moment before responding, 'I'm thinking about trying to control where the fire goes – maybe I can move it from place to place, or make it bigger or smaller.'

Local inventors are already buzzing with ideas about how to build on Thag's discovery. Some suggest using sticks and twine to keep a fire going in a controlled way, while others dream of making portable fires for cooking on the go. There's even talk of using fire to create new tools by heating rocks to mould them into new shapes.

Conclusion

It's clear that Thag Flintfoot's discovery has sparked a revolution in the Stone Age. With fire now at humanity's fingertips, the possibilities for how it will shape Stone Age life are endless. From cooking to warmth to protection from wild animals, Thag's invention may well be remembered as one of the greatest achievements in history.

4 THE STONE AGE TIMES
✏ SIMPLE QUESTIONS

Look at the paragraph beginning...

1. 'In what can only be described as...'
   How can you tell that the discovery was a surprise for the community?

   _____

2. 'The implications of Thag's discovery are enormous.'
   Why do you think cooking with fire was a big change for Thag?

   _____

3. 'I threw some meat on the flames...'
   How can you tell that mealtimes took a long time before the discovery of fire?

   _____

4. 'But the benefits don't stop at the dinner table.'
   Why do you think fire was useful for keeping warm?

   _____

5. 'I had some wolves circling the camp...'
   How do you know fire helped protect Thag's camp?

   _____

6 'Thag's fellow tribespeople are still wrapping their heads around the discovery...'
Why do you think some people in the tribe were excited about fire?

_____

7 'Bora Rocksmash, a respected elder...'
How can you tell that Bora was worried about using fire?

_____

8 'When asked about his future plans...'
Why do you think Thag wanted to control the fire better?

_____

9 'Some suggest using sticks and twine...'
How can you tell that others in the tribe wanted to improve Thag's discovery?

_____

10 'There's even talk of using fire to create new tools...'
Why do you think using fire to make tools is important?

_____

4 THE STONE AGE TIMES

SENTENCE INFERENCE

1 'However, not everyone is so sure. Bora Rocksmash, a respected elder of the tribe, is a bit sceptical. 'I'm all for the warmth,' she said, 'but we need to be careful.'

How can you tell that the community listen to Bora Rocksmash's opinion?

_____

2 'I was just banging two stones together, like usual,' he explained, still smelling faintly of smoke. 'Then – whoosh! – there was a spark, and next thing I knew, the dry grass in front of me was on fire!'

What sense do you get from Thag's words? A sense of… Tick **one**.

worry	☐
pride	☐
surprise	☐
boredom	☐

3 'Local inventors are already buzzing with ideas about how to build on Thag's discovery.'

What does the word **'buzzing'** tell you about how the mood of the inventors?

_____

4 'Fire can also be used for warmth, keeping people cosy during cold nights without needing to pile on extra mammoth furs.'

How will fire impact Stone Age life? It will make it more… Tick **one**.

fun	☐
exciting	☐
dangerous	☐
comfortable	☐

5 'Some suggest using sticks and twine to keep a fire going in a controlled way, while others dream of making portable fires for cooking on the go.'

What does the word **'portable'** tell us about what Stone Age people would like to do with fire?

_____

4 THE STONE AGE TIMES
💭 THIS SUGGESTS...

1 'I was just banging two stones together, like usual. Then – whoosh! – there was a spark.' What does this suggest about how Thag discovered fire?

- [ ] Thag was trying to create fire.
- [ ] Thag found fire accidentally.
- [ ] Thag was afraid of fire.

2 'I threw some meat on the flames, and it came out all crispy on the outside but soft in the middle.'
What does this suggest about Thag's thoughts on cooked meat?

- [ ] Thag thought it was too hard to eat.
- [ ] Thag didn't like the taste.
- [ ] Thag thought it was easier to eat.

3 '...when they saw the fire, they ran off. I think they're afraid of it.'
What does this suggest about the effect of fire on wild animals?

- [ ] Fire attracts animals.
- [ ] Fire scares animals away.
- [ ] Fire makes animals hungry.

4 'Me tired of cold nights and raw food.'
What does this suggest about Oog's feelings toward fire?

- [ ] Oog doesn't care about fire.
- [ ] Oog is glad to have fire.
- [ ] Oog is afraid of fire.

4 THE STONE AGE TIMES

🔍 EVIDENCE – TWO MARKS

Look at the paragraph beginning...

1 'According to Thag…'
How can you tell that Thag was surprised by the fire he created? Give **two** ways.

1 _____

2 _____

2 'I threw some meat on the flames…'
How can you tell that Thag was pleased with the way cooked meat tasted? Give **two** ways.

1 _____

2 _____

3 'Thag's fellow tribespeople are still...'
Why do you think Oog is excited about the discovery of fire? Give **two** ways.

1 _____

2 _____

4 'However, not everyone is so sure.'
How can you tell that Bora Rocksmash thinks fire can be dangerous? Give **two** ways.

1 _____

2 _____

4 THE STONE AGE TIMES

🔍 EVIDENCE – THREE MARKS

1 Look at the whole text. Give **three** pieces of evidence that show Bora is cautious about using fire.

1 _____

_____

_____

2 _____

_____

_____

3 _____

_____

_____

4 THE STONE AGE TIMES

🔍 EVIDENCE – THREE MARKS

2 What impression do you get of Thag's feelings about discovering fire? Give **two** impressions, using evidence from the text to support your answer.

Impression	Evidence

3 What impression do you get of Bora's feelings about fire? Give **two** impressions, using evidence from the text to support your answer.

Impression	Evidence

4 THE STONE AGE TIMES
SUMMARY AND PREDICTION

SUMMARISE

1 What statement best describes the overall impact of Thag's discovery on his tribe?

The tribe sees fire as dangerous and unnecessary. ☐

The tribe is excited but also cautious about fire. ☐

The tribe doesn't understand why fire is important. ☐

2 What best describes the differing attitudes of Thag and Bora towards fire?

Thag is excited about the new uses of fire, while Bora is cautious about its dangers. ☐

Both Thag and Bora are eager to use fire for warmth and cooking. ☐

Thag and Bora think fire is too dangerous to use regularly. ☐

SEQUENCE

3 Number the following sentences from 1–4 to show the order they happen in the text. The first one has been done for you.

Thag accidentally creates a spark by banging two stones together. **1**

Thag tries cooking meat over the fire, finding it tastier. ☐

Thag realises the fire is warm and can be useful. ☐

The dry grass catches fire in front of Thag. ☐

PREDICTION

4 What is most likely to happen in Thag's tribe now that they have discovered fire? Tick **one**.

They will experiment with cooking different foods to improve their meals. ☐

They will spend more time around the fire, building a stronger sense of community. ☐

They will use fire to scare away rival tribes and protect their territory. ☐

AVA'S GONE AND PETS IN CLASS

JOSHUA SEIGAL

Ava's Gone

I look and see
a hole in the class where she used to be.
They told us she'd be gone a while
but it's been six weeks since I saw her smile.

I've asked the teacher every day
when she'll be back, but he won't say.
I've asked my mum, who doesn't know
and so I feel her absence grow

and fester as I sit alone.
I'm weighted down by this heavy stone.
The playground isn't as it was.
The halls are hollowed out because

My best friend's gone. I sigh and see
a hole in my world where she used to be.

Pets in Class

Our teacher let us bring our pets
to class for show and tell.
Alas, however, this endeavour
didn't go too well.

It wasn't funny when my bunny
gnawed right through my books,
and when my pug attacked the rug
we got some awkward looks.

Dan's Dalmation dealt damnation
everywhere it dashed.
Belle's Belgian Hare upset a chair
while ornaments were smashed.

Ravinder's rat (an acrobat)
leapt up to grab the light,
and Eric's ferrets brought no merits
when they had a fight.

But I can say, despite today,
our teacher's room is fine,
for the misrule was not at school:
our lesson was online.

5 AVA'S GONE AND PETS IN CLASS

SIMPLE QUESTIONS

Look at *Ava's Gone*.

1. Why do you think the narrator is feeling sad?

   _____

2. Why do you think the teacher won't give the narrator an answer?

   _____

3. How can you tell that the narrator is feeling emotional?

   _____

4. Why do you think the playground feels different to the narrator?

   _____

5. How can you tell that Ava is very important to the narrator?

   _____

Look at *Pets in Class*.

6 How can you tell that the bunny caused a problem?

_____

7 How can you tell that Dan's Dalmation was hard to control?

_____

8 How do you think the hare 'upset' the chair?

_____

9 Why do you think Eric might not be very happy with how his ferrets behaved?

_____

10 Why did the teacher's room stay tidy?

_____

5 AVA'S GONE AND PETS IN CLASS

SENTENCE INFERENCE

1 'They told us she'd be gone a while
but it's been six weeks since I saw her smile.'

How is the narrator feeling about Ava?

_____

2 'I'm weighted down by this heavy stone.'
What does this tell us about the strength of the narrator's feelings?

_____

3 'It wasn't funny when my bunny
gnawed right through my books,…'

What does the word **'gnawed'** tell you about what the bunny has done to the books?

_____

4 'But I can say, despite today,
our teacher's room is fine,'

What do you think the teacher feels at the end of the poem? A sense of… Tick **one**.

happiness ☐
frustration ☐
relief ☐
anger ☐

5 'and when my pug attacked the rug
we got some awkward looks.'
What do the class think about the narrator's pug? Tick **one**.

They're impressed by the pug. ☐
They're surprised by the pug. ☐
They're afraid of the pug. ☐
They think the pug is cute. ☐

5 AVA'S GONE AND PETS IN CLASS
THIS SUGGESTS...

1. 'I've asked the teacher every day when she'll be back, but he won't say.'
   What does this suggest about how the narrator feels?

   The narrator feels hopeless. ☐

   The narrator is content. ☐

   The narrator is hopeful. ☐

2. 'The playground isn't as it was.'
   What does this suggest about how the narrator views their time at school?

   They feel lonely. ☐

   They feel bored. ☐

   They feel happy. ☐

3. 'Ravinder's rat (an acrobat)
   leapt up to grab the light.'
   What does this suggest about Ravinder's rat?

   The rat is quite lazy. ☐

   The rat is talented and can jump. ☐

   The rat is scary and fierce. ☐

4. 'Dan's Dalmation dealt damnation
   everywhere it dashed.'
   What does this suggest about the Dalmatian's behaviour?

   The Dalmatian is calm. ☐

   The Dalmatian is playful. ☐

   The Dalmatian is destructive. ☐

5 AVA'S GONE AND PETS IN CLASS

🔍 EVIDENCE – TWO MARKS

Look at the poem:

1 *Ava's Gone*
How can you tell that the narrator feels lonely? Give **two** ways.

1 _____

2 _____

2 *Ava's Gone*
How can you tell that Ava might not return to school? Give **two** ways.

1 _____

2 _____

3 *Pets in Class*
How can you tell that the narrator was not impressed by their pets? Give **two** ways.

1 _____

2 _____

4 *Pets in Class*
How can you tell that the pets caused chaos during the lesson? Give **two** ways.

1 _____

2 _____

5 AVA'S GONE AND PETS IN CLASS

🔍 EVIDENCE – THREE MARKS

1 Look at *Pets in Class*. Give **three** examples of how the pets caused problems during show and tell.

1 _____

_____

_____

2 _____

_____

_____

3 _____

_____

_____

5 AVA'S GONE AND PETS IN CLASS

🔍 EVIDENCE – THREE MARKS

2 What impression do you get of Ava in *Ava's Gone*? Give **two** impressions, using evidence from the text to support your answer.

Impression	Evidence

3 In *Pets in Class*, what impression do you get about the pets that came to class? Give **two** impressions, using evidence from the text to support your answer.

Impression	Evidence

5 AVA'S GONE AND PETS IN CLASS

SUMMARY AND PREDICTION

SUMMARISE

1 What best describes the narrator's feelings about Ava's absence?

- The narrator is confused about why Ava left. ☐
- The narrator is excited for Ava to return soon. ☐
- The narrator feels lonely and misses Ava deeply. ☐

2 What best describes the outcome of the show-and-tell activity in *Pets in Class*?

- The pets caused chaos, the teacher was relieved. ☐
- The pets behaved well, impressing the teacher. ☐
- The activity ended early because the teacher was angry. ☐

SEQUENCE

3 Number the following sentences from 1–4 to show the order they happen in the text. The first one has been done for you.

- Dan's Dalmatian causes destruction wherever it goes. `1`
- Ravinder's rat leaps to grab the light. ☐
- Eric's ferrets start fighting. ☐
- Belle's Belgian Hare knocks over a chair and ornaments. ☐

PREDICTION

4 What is most likely to happen next in *Ava's Gone*? Tick **one**.

- Ava returns to the school the next day. ☐
- The narrator makes a new best friend. ☐
- The teacher announces that Ava has gone away permanently. ☐

Comprehension Ninja Inference and Beyond © Andrew Jennings, 2025

KID NORMAL

GREG JAMES AND CHRIS SMITH

Murph and Billy are already in trouble after 'The Great Tomato Sauce Incident'. They head to the library to escape the cold. Then the dreaded Mr Flash arrives…

…Mr Flash barged into the library like a wrecking ball.

'COOPER!' he barked, looking around like an angry lighthouse.

Mrs Fletcher bristled. 'Shhhhhhh,' she hissed sharply.

Mr Flash tried again. 'COOPER!' he husked, in one of the loudest whispers ever recorded.

'Oh nooooo,' whined Billy, sliding down behind his chair, 'he's gonna shout at us. He's still angry about getting covered in saaaaaauce.' But it wasn't sauce that Mr Flash had come to discuss. He spotted Murph in his seat beside the window and strode over, his huge boots clonking on the floor. Mrs Fletcher went bright pink and made another angry shushing noise.

'Cooper,' began Mr Flash in an even more strangled voice. 'I have some news for you. Now that I've got to start preparing the class for their P-CAT, obviously there's not much point you being in my lessons.'

Oh great, thought Murph. *This is where he tells me I can hang out in the library for an hour every morning.*

'But you're not going to be hanging about in the library every morning,' roared Mr Flash unhelpfully. Behind him, Mrs Fletcher got up from her librarian's chair, looking furious and shushing like a nearly boiled kettle. 'You're going to be helping out Carl while the rest of us have CT.' Mr Flash looked like he was enjoying himself enormously.

'The caretaker?' asked Murph blankly.

'That's right. You'll be the right-hand man's right-hand man,' Mr Flash went on. 'So in the morning, you head to Carl's and see what you can help out with, and leave the rest of us to get on with some work. ALL RIGHT?'

Mr Flash had gradually become aware that someone was standing right beside him, breathing heavily. Nervously, he turned his head and found himself staring into the furious eyes of Mrs Fletcher.

'This is a library,' she began angrily, 'and I … said … shush. So would you please … shush.'

'All right, Mrs Mouse, just giving Cooper here some good news. Keep your knickers on.'

'I beg your pardon …' began Mrs Fletcher.

'You heard. Don't get your hair in a twist. It's too quiet in here anyway.'

At this point Mrs Fletcher lost her temper. And this is where Murph found out what her Capability was. Because when Mrs Fletcher boils over, her head transforms into a very large foghorn. And you know what noise a very large foghorn makes.

'PAAAAAAAAARP!' went Mrs Fletcher's foghorn head, directly into Mr Flash's face.

And then again. Twice more. 'PAAAAAAAARP! PAAAAAAARP!'

After the three blasts, the entire library was silent from shock and awe.

Mr Flash looked rather dazed and rather windswept. He reached up and wiped some librarian spit off his face, adjusted his moustache and quietly walked off.

Mrs Fletcher's head transformed back into a normal-sized librarian head and she sat down as if nothing had happened.

6 KID NORMAL

✏️ SIMPLE QUESTIONS

Look at the paragraph beginning...

1. 'A couple of weeks after the Great Tomato Sauce Incident, Murph and Billy had wandered to the library.'
   Why do Murph and Billy choose to go to the library?

   _____

2. 'Mr Flash barged into the library like a wrecking ball.'
   How do you think Mr Flash was feeling when he came into the library?

   _____

3. 'But you're not going to be hanging about...'
   How can you tell Mr Flash likes sending Murph to Carl?

   _____

4. 'Mrs Fletcher bristled.'
   Why is Mrs Fletcher annoyed with Mr Flash?

   _____

5. 'Mr Flash had gradually become aware that...'
   Why does Mr Flash look nervous?

   _____

6 'I have some news for you. Now that I've got to start preparing the class for their P-CAT…'
How does Murph feel when he finds out he won't be in Mr Flash's lessons anymore?

_____

7 'Mr Flash had gradually become aware that…'
How can he tell that someone is right beside him?

_____

8 'You heard.'
Why do you think Mrs Fletcher becomes even angrier with Mr Flash?

_____

9 'After three blasts…'
How did the other people in the library react to Mrs Fletcher's foghorn moment?

_____

10 'All right, Mrs Mouse, just giving Cooper here some good news.'
Why do you think Mr Flash calls Mrs Fletcher 'Mrs Mouse'?

_____

6 KID NORMAL

SENTENCE INFERENCE

1 'Behind him, Mrs Fletcher got up from her librarian's chair, looking furious and shushing like a nearly boiled kettle.'

Why does this sentence describe Mrs Fletcher as a **'nearly boiled kettle'**?

_____

2 'Oh nooooo,' whined Billy, sliding down behind his chair, 'he's gonna shout at us.'

What does the phrase **'sliding down his chair tell'** us about how Billy is feeling? Tick **one**.

happy ☐
unsafe ☐
worried ☐
angry ☐

3 'This is a library,' she began angrily, 'and I … said … shush. So would you please … shush.'

What does Mrs Fletcher's response to Mr Flash tell us about her character?

_____

4 'The caretaker?' asked Murph blankly.'

What does the word **'blankly'** tell you about Murph's reaction to helping the caretaker?

_____

5 'Mr Flash looked rather dazed and rather windswept. He reached up and wiped some librarian spit off his face, adjusted his moustache and quietly walked off.'

What does this tell us about how Mr Flash felt after Mrs Fletcher's foghorn reaction? Tick **one**.

He felt furious. ☐
He felt surprised. ☐
He felt happy. ☐
He felt proud. ☐

6 KID NORMAL
💭 THIS SUGGESTS…

1 'Mrs Fletcher bristled. 'Shhhhhhh,' she hissed sharply.'
What does this suggest about Mrs Fletcher's feelings about noise in the library?

- She likes it when people talk loudly. ☐
- She wants the library to stay quiet. ☐
- She doesn't care about the noise. ☐

2 'Because when Mrs Fletcher boils over, her head transforms into a very large foghorn.'
What does this suggest about Mrs Fletcher's reaction to Mr Flash?

- She gets very angry when someone is noisy. ☐
- She thinks Mr Flash is funny. ☐
- She feels scared of Mr Flash. ☐

3 '…leave the rest of us to get on with some work. ALL RIGHT?'
What does this suggest about Mr Flash's view of Murph as a student?

- He thinks Murph is hardworking. ☐
- He thinks Murph disrupts the lessons. ☐
- He thinks Murph should teach the class. ☐

4 'Mr Flash looked like he was enjoying himself enormously.'
What does this suggest about Mr Flash's feelings towards Murph helping Carl?

- He thinks Murph and Carl will become great friends. ☐
- He likes the idea of punishing Murph. ☐
- He wants Murph to learn a new skill. ☐

6 KID NORMAL

🔍 EVIDENCE – TWO MARKS

Look at the whole text...

1 How can you tell that Mr Flash doesn't respect Mrs Fletcher? Give **two** ways.

1 _____

_____

2 _____

_____

2 'COOPER!' he barked...'
How can you tell that Mr Flash is about to bring bad news to Murph Cooper? Give **two** ways.

1 _____

_____

2 _____

_____

3 Look at the whole text. How can you tell that Mr Flash doesn't like teaching Murph? Give **two** ways.

1 _____

_____

2 _____

_____

4 Look at the whole text. How can you tell that Murph is not expecting his new role with the caretaker? Give **two** ways.

1 _____

_____

2 _____

_____

6 KID NORMAL

🔍 EVIDENCE – THREE MARKS

1 Look at the whole text. How can you tell that Mr Flash is unkind? Give **three** ways.

1 _____

_____

_____

2 _____

_____

_____

3 _____

_____

_____

6 KID NORMAL

🔍 EVIDENCE – THREE MARKS

2 What impression do you get of Billy? Give **two** impressions using evidence from the text to support your answer.

Impression	Evidence

3 What impression do you get of Mrs Fletcher from her actions in the library? Give **two** impressions using evidence from the text to support your answer.

Impression	Evidence

6 KID NORMAL
🔮 SUMMARY AND PREDICTION

SUMMARISE

1 What best describes how Murph feels when Mr Flash talks to him?

nervous and worried ☐

angry and upset ☐

proud and confident ☐

2 What statement best describes Mrs Fletcher's library?

It's a place for friends to talk. ☐

It's a place for silent reading. ☐

It's a place to eat snacks. ☐

SEQUENCE

3 Number the following sentences from 1–4 to show the order they happen in the text. The first one has been done for you.

Billy and Murph enter the library. ☐

Mrs Fletcher's head transforms. ☐

The Great Tomato Sauce incident. `1`

Mr Flash stomps over to Murph. ☐

PREDICTION

4 Do you think Murph will make a lot of noise in the library in the future? Tick **one**.

Murph will feel confident talking loudly to Billy in the library. ☐

Murph will be too scared of Mrs Fletcher to make any noise. ☐

Murph will get on well with Mrs Fletcher and talk to her a lot. ☐

WILDSMITH: INTO THE DARK FOREST

LIZ FLANAGAN

Chapter 7

Full of excitement and determination, Rowan darted along the path and right into the Dark Forest.

Trees towered over her, their leaves filtering the light to make a soft green shade beneath their branches. Birds called. Creatures rustled through the tangle of grasses and thorny vines.

It was beautiful. As she walked through the soft grass, dotted with flowers, Rowan had the strangest feeling that she had come home, finally. There were so many different trees arching overhead. She recognised oak and beech and holly, and her namesake – the rowan tree. Right now the rowan was covered in beautiful blossom, but it would have red berries in the autumn. The name suited her, everyone said, because her hair was bright orange-red, the same colour as the ripening fruit, and her skin was creamy white, like the blossom.

She came to a clearing, edged in rocks.

Rowan sniffed. She could smell burning.

She saw that the bushes and trees at the far edge of the clearing had been scorched. Some branches were blackened; others hung down as if something had torn them off. 'What happened here?' she whispered to herself.

She turned slowly, seeing the damage to the trees, the crushed grass, as if something enormous had been dragged along the floor. There were even deep claw marks.

It looked as if something huge had been in a fight. But she knew there were no animals that big, except in stories. Then she remembered the loud noise she'd been hearing since they arrived, and the way Grandpa and Mum has reacted strangely. What kind of animal made a sound like that, louder than a bellowing bull?

What weren't they telling her about the Dark Forest? Just then, she spotted a patch of smouldering grass. Rowan put her hand out and felt the heat rising up from the ground. 'What could do this? I don't understand.' Again, she got the strangest feeling that someone needed help. Someone close by. Her heart started beating faster as she looked all around her.

There, by her foot, was a piece of eggshell. She picked it up: it was large and curved and emerald green. Too big to belong to any bird.

She walked round the edge of the clearing, trying to understand for herself what had happened here. Just then, she heard a noise, a bit like a squeaky door.

Mrrrr-eeeep. She followed the sound.

It came again, something like a cat in distress.

She climbed a large rock, listening hard and peered down behind it.

Rowan saw a flash of green scales. Was it a snake? She bent down to look closer. 'Oh!' She recognised the creature from her story books.

A green dragon was staring back at her. It looked very small and very scared.

Rowan stared in astonishment, hardly able to believe what she was seeing.

Chapter 8

The dragon huddled down, looking afraid. One of its wings was twisted. It made a hissing sound and tried to flap its wings. It must be injured because it cried even louder. 'It's alright, little one, I won't hurt you,' she told it.

Dragons were real! Amazed, Rowan drank in the sight of this magical creature.

The dragon was bright grass-green, covered in shiny scales. It had two long pointed ears, large yellow eyes and four strong little limbs, with tiny spines all down its back and tail.

Rowan felt a surge of protectiveness and love for the baby dragon. Without stopping to think, she reached down and picked it up, cuddling it close to her chest. With her free hand, she stroked the dragon's head. It felt cool and smooth. It blinked once and then closed its eyes.

'You're beautiful, aren't you?' she told it gently. 'I'm sorry you're hurt. My Grandpa's a healer,' she whispered. 'So maybe he can fix your wing. But first, let's try and find your mum.' She looked around for more signs of a large dragon. Which way had it gone? Remembering those claw marks, she began to retrace her steps.

She'd only just left the clearing when she heard raised voices. Rowan stepped behind a broad oak tree, staying hidden, and peered carefully through its leaves. Just a few strides ahead, there were a handful of strangers dragging a huge net along the floor. These people were armed with spears, bows and arrows. They must be hunting, even though Rowan hadn't seen any deer or rabbits or pheasants today.

7 WILDSMITH: INTO THE DARK FOREST

✎ SIMPLE QUESTIONS

Look at the paragraph beginning...

1 'Full of excitement and determination...'
How can you tell that Rowan is moving quickly?

_____

2 'It was beautiful.'
How can you tell that Rowan feels a connection to the forest?

_____

3 'She saw that the bushes and trees...'
Why do you think Rowan is curious about the clearing?

_____

4 'It looked as if something huge had been in a fight.'
How can you tell that Rowan is confused about what she sees?

_____

5 'Rowan put her hand out.'
Why do you think Rowan is concerned about the smouldering grass?

_____

6 'There, by her foot.'
How can you tell that the eggshell is unusual?

_____

7 'It came again…'
Why do you think Rowan follows the *'Mrrrr-eeeep'* sound?

_____

8 'The dragon huddled down.'
How can you tell that the dragon wants to run away?

_____

9 'Rowan felt a surge of protectiveness.'
How can you tell that the dragon feels happy with Rowan picking it up?

_____

10 'She'd only just left the clearing…'
How can you tell that Rowan feels cautious around the strangers?

_____

7 WILDSMITH: INTO THE DARK FOREST

✪ SENTENCE INFERENCE

1 'Trees towered over her, their leaves filtering the light to make a soft green shade beneath their branches.'

What does the word **'towered'** tell you about the trees?

_____

2 'Without stopping to think, she reached down and picked it up, cuddling it close to her chest. With her free hand, she stroked the dragon's head.'

What can we tell about Rowan's nature from this passage? She is… Tick **one**.

- angry ☐
- strong ☐
- daring ☐
- protective ☐

3 'What weren't they telling her about the Dark Forest?'

What does the name of the forest tell you about it?

_____

4 'The dragon huddled down, looking afraid. One of its wings was twisted. It made a hissing sound and tried to flap its wings.'

How is the dragon feeling? Tick **one**.

- threatened ☐
- tired ☐
- angry ☐
- furious ☐

5 'Remembering those claw marks, she began to retrace her steps.'

What does this sentence tell you about what Rowan did?

_____

7 WILDSMITH: INTO THE DARK FOREST
💭 THIS SUGGESTS…

1 'Rowan had the strangest feeling that she had come home, finally.'
What does this suggest about how Rowan feels about the Dark Forest?

- Rowan feels scared of the forest. ☐
- Rowan feels connected to the forest. ☐
- Rowan feels lost in the forest. ☐

2 'She saw that the bushes and trees at the far edge of the clearing had been scorched.'
What does this suggest about what happened in the clearing?

- There was a fire or something burned the trees. ☐
- People have cut down the trees. ☐
- The trees are dying naturally. ☐

3 'There, by her foot, was a piece of eggshell. She picked it up: it was large and curved and emerald green.'
What does this suggest about the eggshell?

- It belongs to a bird. ☐
- It is unusual and could belong to a magical creature. ☐
- It is just a rock shaped like an egg. ☐

4 'Just a few strides ahead, there were a handful of strangers dragging a huge net along the floor.'
What does this suggest about the strangers?

- They are lost in the forest. ☐
- They have been hunting something. ☐
- They are helping Rowan find the dragon. ☐

⑦ WILDSMITH: INTO THE DARK FOREST

🔍 EVIDENCE – TWO MARKS

Look at the paragraph beginning...

1 'Rowan had the strangest feeling that she had come home, finally.' How can you tell that Rowan feels connected to the Dark Forest? Give **two** ways.

1 _____

2 _____

2 'Rowan felt a surge of protectiveness and love for the baby dragon.' How can you tell that Rowan cares about the dragon? Give **two** ways.

1 _____

2 _____

3 'Just a few strides ahead, there were a handful of strangers dragging a huge net along the floor.' How can you tell that the strangers might be dangerous? Give **two** ways.

1 _____

2 _____

4 'There, by her foot, was a piece of eggshell.' How can you tell that the eggshell is unusual? Give **two** ways.

1 _____

2 _____

7 WILDSMITH: INTO THE DARK FOREST

🔍 EVIDENCE – THREE MARKS

1 'Just a few strides ahead, there were a handful of strangers dragging a huge net.' How can you tell that Rowan is cautious around the strangers?

1 _____

2 _____

3 _____

⑦ WILDSMITH: INTO THE DARK FOREST

🔍 EVIDENCE – THREE MARKS

2 What impression do you get of Rowan's attitude toward the baby dragon? Give **two** impressions, using evidence from the text to support your answer.

Impression	Evidence

3 What impression do you get of Rowan's personality from her actions in the Dark Forest? Give **two** impressions, using evidence from the text to support your answer:

Impression	Evidence

7 WILDSMITH: INTO THE DARK FOREST

SUMMARY AND PREDICTION

SUMMARISE

1 What best describes the atmosphere of the Dark Forest?

The Dark Forest feels calm and magical. ☐

The Dark Forest feels dangerous and threatening. ☐

The Dark Forest feels bright and cheerful. ☐

2 What best describes Rowan's impression of the dragon?

Rowan thinks the dragon is dangerous and scary. ☐

Rowan thinks the dragon is beautiful and needs her help. ☐

Rowan thinks the dragon is annoying and a burden. ☐

SEQUENCE

3 Number the following sentences from 1–4 to show the order they happen in the text. The first one has been done for you.

Rowan becomes curious as she notices the claw marks and scorched ground. ☐

Rowan grows cautious when she hears strangers dragging a net nearby. ☐

Rowan feels excited as she enters the forest, taking in its beauty. ☐ 1

Rowan feels protective when she discovers the injured baby dragon. ☐

PREDICTION

4 What is most likely to be in the hunters' net? Tick **one**.

A large deer they caught earlier. ☐

The baby dragon's mother. ☐

Nothing; the net is empty. ☐

THE JOURNEY OF RUBY THE RED BLOOD CELL

ANDREW JENNINGS

Date: Day 1,054 of my journey

Dear Diary,

Today marks another exciting chapter in my life as Ruby the Red Blood Cell! It's been quite the adventure since I was born among the bustling bone marrow. That's when I learned my purpose: to carry oxygen to every corner of the body. Each day is a new experience, filled with the thrill of discovery.

First Stop: The Heart!

My journey began in the left atrium of the heart, a cosy chamber where I felt safe among other newly formed cells. With a gentle contraction, I was pushed through the mitral valve into the left ventricle. It was such an electric moment! The muscle around me flexed, and sent me flying into the aorta, which felt like being on a roller coaster ride. Adrenaline rushed through my tiny membrane! The aorta, the largest blood vessel, was like a grand highway, and I was ready to zoom down the path of life.

Through the Arteries

As I raced through the arteries, I felt the pulse of life reverberating around me. The smooth, elastic walls of the vessels guided me like a swift current, and I revelled in the speed. I passed white blood cells with their vigilant eyes, and platelets, ready to mend any injury. We all had our own missions and important roles in this intricate dance of life. I was determined to deliver my precious cargo: oxygen!

Arriving in the Lungs

After an exhilarating ride, I arrived at the lungs. I entered the tiny alveoli, the miraculous air sacs where the real magic happens. Here, I exchanged my carbon dioxide for fresh oxygen, the lifeblood of my existence. It felt like a refreshing deep breath after a long swim, revitalising me for the journey ahead. I could sense the vibrant energy around me, knowing I was now fully charged and ready to return to the heart, eager to share the oxygen with the rest of the body.

FICTIONAL DIARY ENTRY

Back to the Heart

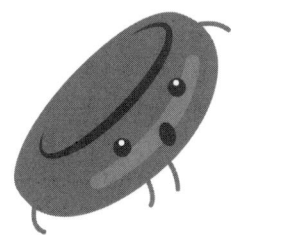

With my new load of oxygen, I made my way back to the heart. I squeezed through the pulmonary veins, entering the right atrium, where I mingled with my fellow cells. The atmosphere buzzed with anticipation as I was drawn into the left ventricle once again. I could feel the excitement in the air – every heartbeat was a reminder of the vital role we played in sustaining life.

Delivering Oxygen

From the heart, I travelled through the arteries to the capillaries, the tiniest blood vessels, where my work truly began. As I slowed down to navigate these narrow spaces, I felt a sense of purpose washing over me. Here, I released the oxygen into the tissues, and it was as if I could hear the cells around me sigh with gratitude as they absorbed the life-giving oxygen. This moment was a powerful reminder of how interconnected we all are; my journey was not just about me, but about every living cell that depended on my delivery.

The Return Journey

Once my job was done, I collected carbon dioxide from the tissues. Then the waste product was carried back to the lungs for exhalation. I followed the veins back to the heart, reflecting on the important exchange that had just taken place. It was humbling to think that while I was a small part of this grand system, I played a crucial role in maintaining the delicate balance of life.

Reflections

As I rest in the heart, preparing for another cycle, I can't help but marvel at the incredible journey I've had. Each day is a new adventure filled with purpose and the thrill of discovery. I'm not just a red blood cell; I'm a vital part of this magnificent system that keeps everything alive. I'm filled with excitement about the countless journeys still ahead.

Until next time, Ruby the Red Blood Cell

8 THE JOURNEY OF RUBY THE RED BLOOD CELL

SIMPLE QUESTIONS

Look at the section titled...

1 'Date: Day 1,054 of my journey'
How can you tell that Ruby enjoys her job as a red blood cell?

_____

2 'First Stop: The Heart!'
Why do you think Ruby compares her journey through the heart to a roller coaster?

_____

3 'Through the Arteries'
How can you tell that Ruby finds her journey through the arteries thrilling?

_____

4 'Arriving in the Lungs'
Why do you think Ruby feels refreshed in the lungs?

_____

5 'Back to the Heart'
How can you tell that Ruby works alongside other cells?

_____

6 'Delivering Oxygen'
How do you know that Ruby feels her job is meaningful?

_____

7 'The Return Journey'
Why do you think Ruby feels humbled during her journey back to the heart?

_____

8 'Reflections'
How can you tell that Ruby is tired after her journey?

_____

9 'The Return Journey'
Why do you think Ruby calls the exchange of oxygen and carbon dioxide an 'important exchange'?

_____

10 'Reflections'
How do you know that Ruby feels positive about the future?

_____

8 THE JOURNEY OF RUBY THE RED BLOOD CELL

SENTENCE INFERENCE

1 'The muscle around me flexed, and sent me flying into the aorta, which felt like being on a roller coaster ride.'

How would you describe the speed that Ruby is moving at?

_____

2 'It was humbling to think that while I was a small part of this grand system, I played a crucial role in maintaining the delicate balance of life.'

What sense does Ruby feel in this passage? A sense of… Tick **one**.

- tiredness ☐
- jealousy ☐
- happiness ☐
- pride ☐

3 'Once my job was done, I collected carbon dioxide from the tissues. Then the waste product was carried back to the lungs for exhalation.'

What does the word **'waste'** tell you about carbon dioxide in the tissue?

_____

4 'It was such an electric moment!'

What emotion is Ruby feeling at this moment? Tick **one**.

- sadness ☐
- fear ☐
- excitement ☐
- happiness ☐

5 'I'm filled with excitement about the countless journeys still ahead.'

What does the word **'countless'** suggest about the journeys that lie ahead?

_____

8 THE JOURNEY OF RUBY THE RED BLOOD CELL

💭 THIS SUGGESTS...

1. 'I'm not just a red blood cell; I'm Ruby, a vital part of this magnificent system that keeps everything alive.' What does this suggest about how Ruby views her role?

   Ruby feels her role is unimportant. ☐

   Ruby thinks she has a key role. ☐

   Ruby thinks her job is boring. ☐

2. 'The moment was electric!' What does this suggest about how Ruby feels during her journey through the heart?

   Ruby feels scared. ☐

   Ruby feels relaxed. ☐

   Ruby finds it exciting. ☐

3. 'I exchanged my carbon dioxide for fresh oxygen, the lifeblood of my existence.' What does this suggest about the importance of oxygen to Ruby?

   Oxygen is not very important. ☐

   Oxygen makes her tired. ☐

   Oxygen is essential for Ruby's role. ☐

4. '...it was as if I could hear the cells around me sigh with gratitude.' What does this suggest about the cells' opinion of Ruby?

   The cells find Ruby annoying. ☐

   The cells are thankful for Ruby's work. ☐

   The cells think Ruby is amazing. ☐

8 THE JOURNEY OF RUBY THE RED BLOOD CELL

🔍 EVIDENCE – TWO MARKS

Look at the section titled...

1. 'Date: Day 1,054 of my journey'
   How can you tell that Ruby is enthusiastic about her role as a red blood cell? Give **two** ways.

   1 _____

   2 _____

2. 'First Stop: The Heart!' How can you tell that Ruby finds her journey through the heart exhilarating? Give **two** ways.

   1 _____

   2 _____

3. 'Through the Arteries.' How can you tell that Ruby values teamwork? Give **two** ways.

   1 _____

   2 _____

4. 'Arriving in the Lungs.' How can you tell that Ruby feels better after reaching the lungs? Give **two** ways.

   1 _____

   2 _____

5. 'Delivering Oxygen.' How can you tell that Ruby feels a strong sense of purpose in delivering oxygen? Give **two** ways.

   1 _____

   2 _____

8 THE JOURNEY OF RUBY THE RED BLOOD CELL

🔍 EVIDENCE – THREE MARKS

1 Give **three** pieces of evidence that show Ruby finds her journey exciting.

1 _____

_____

_____

2 _____

_____

_____

3 _____

_____

_____

8 THE JOURNEY OF RUBY THE RED BLOOD CELL

🔍 EVIDENCE – THREE MARKS

2 How do you think Ruby feels about her role in the body? Give **two** impressions using evidence from the text to support your impressions.

Impression	Evidence

3 What impression do you get of Ruby's experience traveling through the arteries? Give **two** impressions using evidence from the text to support your impressions.

Impression	Evidence

8 THE JOURNEY OF RUBY THE RED BLOOD CELL
SUMMARY AND PREDICTION

SUMMARISE

1 What statement best describes Ruby's attitude towards her role in the body?

Ruby feels her work is boring and unimportant. ☐

Ruby thinks her work is exciting and meaningful. ☐

Ruby feels tired and wishes she could stop working. ☐

2 What statement best describes Ruby's experience traveling through the heart?

Ruby finds the heart scary and dangerous. ☐

Ruby thinks the heart is powerful and thrilling. ☐

Ruby finds the heart too complicated to understand. ☐

SEQUENCE

3 Number the following sentences from 1–4 to show the order they happen in the text. The first one has been done for you.

Ruby exchanges carbon dioxide for fresh oxygen in the lungs. ☐

Ruby travels through the arteries, enjoying the speed of the journey. ☐

Ruby begins her journey in the heart and is pushed into the aorta. ☐ 1

Ruby delivers oxygen to the tissues in the capillaries. ☐

PREDICTION

4 Which of these events is most likely to happen next in Ruby's journey?

Ruby will decide to take a break from her journey. ☐

Ruby will get lost and not make it back to the heart. ☐

Ruby will continue delivering oxygen. ☐

WHERE I LIVE

JOSHUA SEIGAL

Where I Live

The mirror is enormous
and the tabletop is vast.
The curtains are like a sailcloth
set upon a monstrous mast.

The rug is like an ocean
and the bookcase like a tower.
The chairs are monumental
and the cushions make me cower.

The wall is like a mountain
that would take a year to climb.
The hall's completely cavernous,
its grandeur is sublime.

The ceiling's in the heavens
and the light is like the sun.
My life with these surroundings
is both frightening and fun.

But if you were to visit me
your wonder might be scant;
My dwelling is a normal size,
it's just that I'm an ant…

My home is quite conventional;
it's not unique, I swear.
I'm hoping you'll forgive me
for that anty climax there.

Where I Live from *Who Let the Words Out?* © Joshua Seigal 2023. Reproduced with the permission of Bloomsbury Publishing Plc

9

POETRY

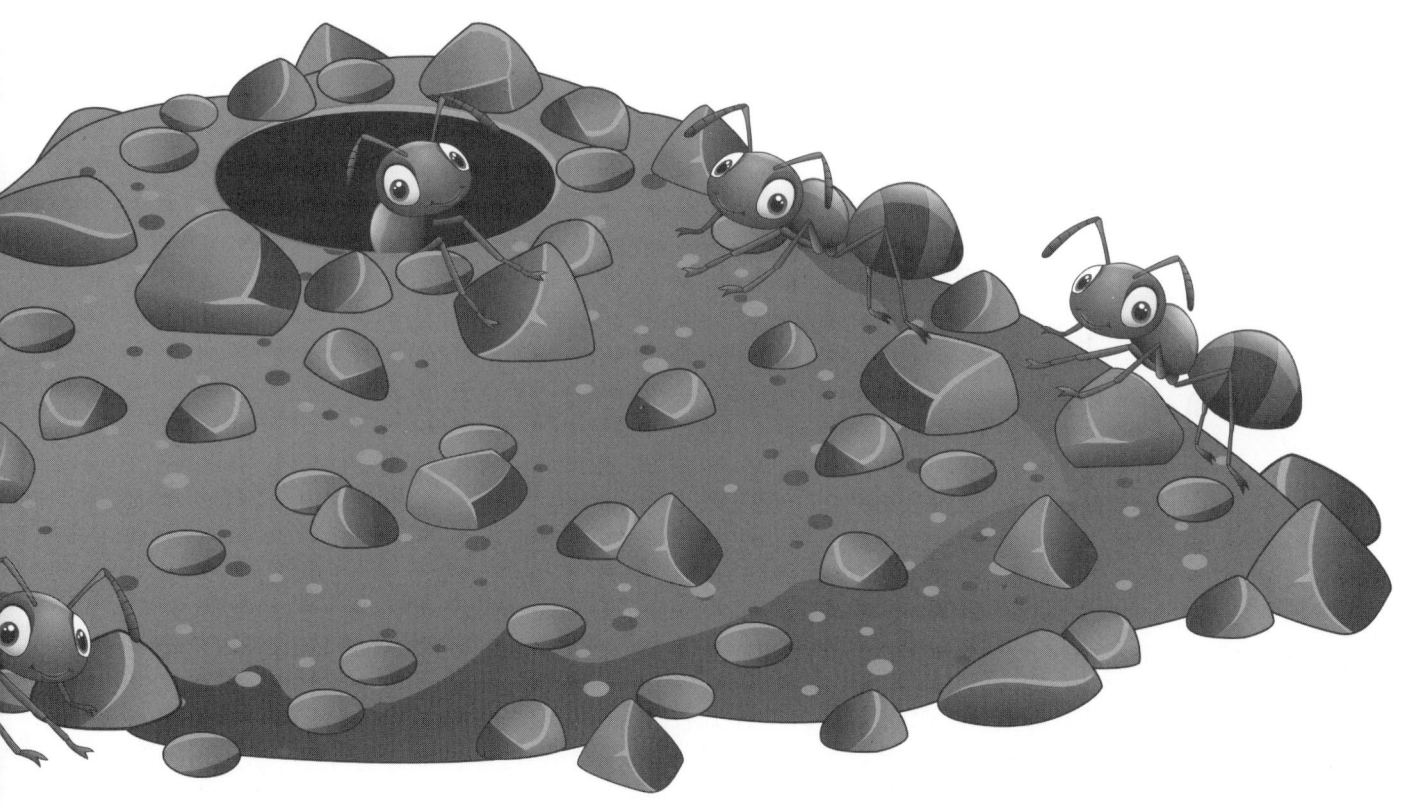

The activities on these pages are about *Where I Live*.

🌀 SIMPLE QUESTIONS

Look at *Where I Live*.

1 Why do you think the narrator describes ordinary objects as enormous?

_____

2 How can you tell that the narrator sometimes feels scared?

_____

3 Why do you think the hall feels so impressive to the narrator?

_____

4 Why does the narrator compare the rug to an ocean?

_____

✳ SENTENCE INFERENCE

1 'My home is quite conventional;
it's not unique, I swear'

What does **'not unique'** tell you about how the ant views their home?

_____

2 'My life with these surroundings,
is both frightening and fun'

How does the narrator feel about where they live? A sense of… Tick **one**.

- curiosity ☐
- calm ☐
- dread ☐
- excitement ☐

😵 THIS SUGGESTS...

'The chairs are monumental
and the cushions make me cower.'
What does this description tell us about how the speaker feels in the room?
Tick **one**.

They feel satisfied. ☐

They feel overwhelmed. ☐

They feel relaxed. ☐

🔍 EVIDENCE

1 How can you tell that the narrator feels small?

   1 _____

   _____

   2 _____

   _____

2 What impression do you get of the narrator's view of their home in *Where I Live*? Give **two** impressions, using evidence from the text to support your answer.

Impression	Evidence

✅ SUMMARY

What does the twist at the end suggest about the narrator's personality?
Tick **one**.

The narrator is serious. ☐

The narrator is playful. ☐

The narrator is cruel. ☐

THE VOICE OF VESUVIUS: A VOLCANO'S TALE

ANDREW JENNINGS

I am Mount Vesuvius, standing tall and proud, watching over the city of Pompeii below. From my peak, I can see everything – the colourful rooftops of houses, the busy markets filled with people, and the sparkling Bay of Naples, shining like a mirror under the bright sun.

Every day, I witness the lively dance of life. Children run through the streets, their laughter rising to me like songs on the wind. Merchants call out, selling bread and fruit, and the scents drift up to my summit. Families gather, friends chat, and the people of Pompeii live their days with joy. I bask in their happiness, feeling the warmth of the sun on my slopes and the gentle touch of the breeze.

But as evening falls, something deep inside me stirs – a faint rumble, like the beginning of a restless dream. The people below carry on, unaware of what's building beneath them, but I can feel it – a pressure growing within me, pressing against my rocky heart.

The sky darkens, and the air becomes thick and heavy. I can still hear the sounds of life below, children laughing, families talking, but it feels distant now, overshadowed by the low growl rising from my depths. The earth trembles slightly, a warning I cannot hold back.

FICTION

Then, without further delay, the ground shudders beneath me. The quiet tremor turns into a powerful quake, and I let out a deep, thunderous roar. The city below is shaken, and the people stop in confusion and fear. Panic spreads as the sky fills with ash and smoke, darkening the once-bright landscape.

Chaos erupts in the streets. People run, their eyes wide with terror. I see mothers clutching their children close, fathers looking for shelter, and friends calling out to each other. The laughter I once heard is now replaced with cries of fear. The calm city I watched over is now a scene of confusion and desperation.

Thick clouds of ash pour from my peak, blocking out the light and casting Pompeii into darkness. Fiery rocks shoot into the air, and ash rains down like a thick, suffocating blanket. Some people hesitate, not sure where to go or what to do, while others try to flee, their footsteps frantic on the cobblestone streets.

Inside, my heart aches. I do not wish to harm them. The joy and life I watched each day gave me peace. But the power building within me is unstoppable, and I have no choice. I erupt with all my force, sending ash and smoke spiralling high into the sky, darkening everything below.

As the eruption settles, a heavy silence falls over the land. Pompeii lies beneath a thick blanket of ash. The bright rooftops and bustling markets are hidden, and the once-busy streets are still and quiet. I am left alone, a silent guardian over a city transformed.

I feel the weight of loss. The laughter and life that filled the air are gone, replaced by the silence of a city now frozen in time. I am a volcano – a force of nature, both protector and destroyer. I am here to watch over Pompeii, holding within me the memories of the life that once thrived beneath my watchful gaze.

Now, I stand quietly once more, my slopes cooled and silent. I remember the joy of the city, the voices and laughter that once echoed up to me. Though Pompeii is changed, I remain as its guardian, forever holding the memory of the life, laughter and love that filled the streets before my eruption.

The activities on these pages are about *The Voice of Vesuvius: A Volcano's Tale.*

🌀 SIMPLE QUESTIONS

Look at the paragraph beginning…

1 'I am Mount Vesuvius.'
How can you tell that Vesuvius cares about the people of Pompeii?

_____

2 'But as evening falls.'
How can you tell that something is changing inside Vesuvius?

_____

3 'Chaos erupts in the streets.'
How do you know that the people are scared?

_____

4 'Thick clouds of ash pour from my peak.'
Why do you think the people have trouble escaping?

_____

✦ SENTENCE INFERENCE

1 'Merchants call out, selling bread and fruit, and the scents drift up to my summit. Families gather, friends chat, and the people of Pompeii live their days with joy.'

How do the people who live in Pompeii feel?

_____

2 'Every day, I witness the lively dance of life. Children run through the streets, their laughter rising to me like songs on the wind.'

What sense do you get from this passage about life. A sense of…Tick **one**.

danger ☐
joy ☐
fear ☐
pride ☐

👁 THIS SUGGESTS...

'I watch as the vibrant city is cloaked in a shroud of ash.' What does this suggest about the impact of the eruption on Pompeii? Tick **one**.

Pompeii has been completely covered. ☐

The city is still visible through the ash. ☐

Pompeii is glowing brightly under the ash. ☐

🔍 EVIDENCE

1 'Chaos erupts in the streets.' How can you tell that the people of Pompeii are panicked?

1 _____

_____

2 _____

_____

2 What impression do you get of Vesuvius's feelings as it begins to feel the eruption? Give **two** impressions, using evidence from the text to support your answer.

Impression	Evidence

✅ SUMMARY

What statement best describes how Vesuvius feels about the city of Pompeii? Tick **one**.

Vesuvius is curious about the daily life of Pompeii's people. ☐

Vesuvius feels a sense of pride in watching over Pompeii. ☐

Vesuvius finds Pompeii too noisy and chaotic. ☐

ISADORA MOON HAS A SLEEPOVER

HARRIET MUNCASTER

'Goodnight, girls,' she said, turning off the light and closing the door. 'Sleep well!'

'Night, Mum,' said Zoe.

We lay there in the dark for a bit, although it wasn't properly dark because Zoe had a nightlight plugged into the wall.

'We need to stay awake,' she whispered, 'so that we can get up for a midnight feast!'

'Ooh yes,' I said. 'What shall we have?'

'Cake,' suggested Zoe, giggling.

'We can't eat the cake!'

'I know – I was only joking. We'll have to find something else. Maybe we can eat the rest of the sprinkles…'

'Maybe,' I said, my mind drifting back to the cake. I was starting to feel a little bit bad. I kept thinking of Oliver and Bruno, and how excited they had been about their dinosaur cake. I knew they would have put a lot of hard work into it.

'Zoe,' I whispered.

'What?'

'I don't think we should enter our cake in the competition.'

'Why not?' said Zoe, sitting bolt upright in the bed. 'Of course we should enter our cake!'

'But we cheated,' I said. 'We used magic. I've been thinking about it all evening. I don't think it would be fair!'

'It was only a little bit of magic,' said Zoe, in a quiet voice.

'It was more than a little bit,' I said. 'And, really, we shouldn't have used any at all. We were having so much fun that we got carried away.'

'But we HAVE to enter the cake,' said Zoe again. 'We want to meet Whippy McFluff, don't we?'

'Well, yes…' I said. 'I just –'

FICTION

'Oh I really want to win and meet Whippy McFluff,' said Zoe, starting to sound a bit upset.

'OK,' I sighed, not wanting to ruin the sleepover with an argument. I tried to change the subject instead.

'How are we going to keep ourselves awake?,' I asked. 'For the midnight feast?'

'By telling ghost stories!' said Zoe, perking up again and giving a little shiver. She lit a torch and put it under her chin.

'I'll start,' she said, and she began to tell a story. It was about an old woman who trailed the streets of our town after dark, dragging chains behind her that clinked and clanked all night long.

'That sounds a bit unrealistic,' I said, thinking about the friendly ghost, Oscar, who lived in my attic at home. 'Let me tell you about my real ghost!'

'But Oscar's not scary,' said Zoe.

'Ghost stories have to be scary. That's the point of them.'

'Oh,' I said, confused.

'Never mind,' said Zoe. 'Let's talk about our biggest wishes instead. Do you know what mine is?'

'To meet Whippy McFluff?'

'Close, but no,' said Zoe. 'My biggest wish is that we can stay best friends for ever! And when we grow up, we can live in houses next door to each other.'

'Oh Zoe,' I said. 'That's a lovely wish! I hope it comes true.'

Zoe smiled and hugged Coco, who was snuggled up in her arms.

'What's yours?' she asked. 'We need to keep talking, so we can stay awake until midnight.'

'Hmm,' I said, 'let me just think about it.' The room went quiet for a moment, and all I could hear was the tick-tock of the clock.

The activities on these pages are about *Isadora Moon Has a Sleepover*.

🌙 SIMPLE QUESTIONS

Look at the paragraph beginning...

1 'Goodnight, girls.'
How can you tell that Zoe and Isadora were excited about staying awake?

_____

2 "Zoe", I whispered.'
How can you tell that Isadora felt guilty about using magic on the cake?

_____

3 'By telling ghost stories!'
Why do you think Zoe wanted to tell scary ghost stories?

_____

4 'Close, but no.'
How can you tell that Zoe values her friendship with Isadora?

_____

✪ SENTENCE INFERENCE

1 'Maybe,' I said, my mind drifting back to the cake. I was starting to feel a little bit bad. I kept thinking of Oliver and Bruno, and how excited they had been about their dinosaur cake. I knew they would have put a lot of hard work into it.'

Why was Isadora starting to feel a little bit bad?

_____

2 'We lay there in the dark for a bit, although it wasn't properly dark because Zoe had a nightlight plugged into the wall.'

What does the nightlight add? A sense of...Tick **one**.

Fun ☐
Fear ☐
Comfort ☐
Tiredness ☐

😨 THIS SUGGESTS...

'But we cheated,' I said. 'We used magic. I don't think it would be fair!'
What does this suggest about Isadora's feelings? Tick **one**.

She thinks magic is fun. ☐

She feels proud of their cake. ☐

She feels guilty about using magic. ☐

🔍 EVIDENCE

1. 'We need to stay awake,' she whispered.'
   How can you tell that Zoe is excited about having a midnight feast?

   1 _____

   2 _____

2. What impression do you get of Isadora's personality? (what kind of person is she?) Give **two** impressions, using evidence from the text to support your answer.

Impression	Evidence

✅ SUMMARY

What best describes Zoe and Isadora's different thoughts about the cake competition? Tick **one**.

Both Zoe and Isadora are excited to enter the cake into the competition. ☐

Zoe wants to enter the cake, but Isadora feels bad about using magic. ☐

Isadora wants to enter the cake and Zoe doesn't care about winning. ☐

THE WILD WEST

ANDREW JENNINGS

The Wild West: Life, Legends, and Adventure

The Wild West was a time of adventure, discovery and danger during the 1800s. People moved west in search of land, gold and a new life. It wasn't all about cowboys and gunfights, though there were plenty of those! Life was tough, and settlers had to be brave to survive.

Life in the Wild West

Life in the Wild West was challenging. Towns were small, and many people lived in cabins. There weren't many rules, and towns could be dangerous, with outlaws and wild animals threatening homes. Families worked hard to grow food and survive.

The land was vast and difficult. The Great Plains stretched for miles, with few trees or rivers. Summers were hot, and winters were freezing. But the open land offered something valuable… freedom. People moved west for the chance to own land, build farms or start businesses. Many headed to places like California, hoping to strike it rich during the gold rush.

Cowboys and Outlaws

Cowboys were skilled horsemen who herded cattle across long distances. They lived tough lives, often sleeping under the stars as they drove cattle to market. Cowboys became symbols of the Wild West and its rugged spirit.

Not everyone in the Wild West followed the law. Outlaws like Jesse James and Billy the Kid became famous for robbing banks, trains and stagecoaches. They were often hunted by sheriffs and lawmen, such as the legendary Wyatt Earp, who worked to keep order in lawless towns.

Famous Events of the Wild West

The Wild West was shaped by famous events like the California Gold Rush of 1849. When gold was discovered, thousands of people rushed west to find their fortune. New towns appeared overnight, and people from all over the world came to dig for gold. Some became rich, but most realised the Wild West was a hard place to succeed.

Another important event was Custer's Last Stand in 1876. This battle took place between the U.S. Army, led by General George Custer, and Native American tribes. Custer and his men were defeated, which became one of the most famous battles in American history. It showed the tension between settlers and Native Americans fighting to protect their land.

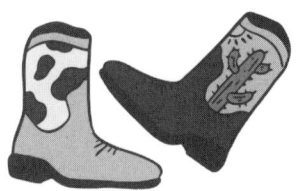

Legendary Figures of the West

The Wild West was full of legendary figures. Annie Oakley was a sharpshooter who could hit targets with amazing accuracy. She travelled with Buffalo Bill's Wild West Show, performing shooting tricks and showing that women in the West were as tough as men.

Buffalo Bill Cody was a buffalo hunter who became famous for his Wild West Show. He travelled across the U.S. and Europe, showing what life in the West was like with rodeos, re-enactments and performances by cowboys and Native Americans.

Calamity Jane was another legend, known for dressing like a man and working as a scout for the army. She became famous for her bravery and wild adventures, with stories about her spreading across the West.

The End of the Wild West

As more people moved west, the Wild West changed. Railroads connected towns, making travel easier. Laws were enforced, and outlaws were captured or killed. Native American tribes were pushed onto reservations, and the wide-open spaces were taken over by farms and cities. By the early 1900s, the Wild West was no more, but its stories and legends live on today.

The activities on these pages are about *The Wild West*.

🖊 SIMPLE QUESTIONS

Look at the paragraph beginning...

1 'Life in the Wild West.'
How can you tell that life was hard for people in the Wild West?

_____

2 'The land was vast and difficult.'
Why do you think people still moved west even though the land was challenging?

_____

3 'Cowboys and Outlaws.'
How do you know that cowboys lived a rough life?

_____

4 Look at the paragraph about outlaws.
Why do you think outlaws like Jesse James became famous?

_____

✪ SENTENCE INFERENCE

1 'The Great Plains stretched for miles, with few trees or rivers. Summers were hot and winters were freezing.'

What does this passage tell us about what life was like in the Wild West?

_____

2 'People moved west for the chance to own land, build farms or start businesses. Many headed to places like California, hoping to strike it rich during the gold rush.'

What sense do you get for why people wanted to move to Wild West?
For a sense of…Tick **one**.

danger ☐
opportunity ☐
adventure ☐
challenge ☐

🌐 THIS SUGGESTS...

'Some became rich, but most realized the Wild West was a hard place to succeed.' What does this suggest about life in the Wild West? Tick **one**.

It was a great place to make money. ☐

Wild West life wasn't suitable for everyone. ☐

It was a comfortable place to live. ☐

🔍 EVIDENCE

1. Look at the 'Legendary Figures of the West' section.
   How do you know that figures like Annie Oakley were admired?

   1 _____
   _____

   2 _____
   _____

2. What impression do you get of life for settlers in the Wild West? Give **two** impressions, using evidence from the text to support your answer.

Impression	Evidence

✅ SUMMARY

After reading the text, what kind of person do you think Annie Oakley was? Tick **one**.

A skilled and bold performer who impressed audiences. ☐

A cautious person who avoided risky situations. ☐

A relaxed person who preferred working indoors. ☐

MY FRIEND THE ALIEN

ZANIB MIAN

Maxx is an alien: a real one - from the planet Zerg. He's on Earth to research these strange things called emotions that humans have.

Day 2

Hey, guys, I'm in a city now, far away from the fields, where there are plenty of humans to watch. I ate my first human food today! It was the most delicious thing I've ever tasted. I got it from a building that was full of all sorts of different things. It's brown and is called Milk Chocolate with Hazelnut Pieces Sainsbury's Taste the Difference. Long name, but tastes awesome. I think I'll be happy if I find nothing else to eat here on Earth other than Milk Chocolate with Hazelnut Pieces Sainsbury's Taste the Difference.

I made my first observation when I was inside that building. Humans release methane too. Though not as much as cows. The place was full of purple gas, which the humans released as they pushed around these metal cages and put things into them. Some of them shouted a lot at the little humans, who seemed to want to put things in the metal cage that the big ones didn't want there. Then a couple of the little ones started making shrieking noises and had water coming out of their eyes. I guess those are feelings; one type of feelings.

I haven't seen the big ones showing many yet. Well, they haven't made any of the shrieking noises. As instructed, I will use the thing called Google to find out more about feelings. By the way, nobody noticed me. Nobody thought I was strange. They don't know I'm not from around here, because I look just like them.

Day 3

Google says these guys have a gazillion different kind of feelings. And they can be soppy, it's unbelievable. The yuckiest one I read about was LOVE. Ewww. I need to get out there, to places where there are lots of humans, to find out how these feelings happen.

In the afternoon, I hopped on a bus, which is an extra-long vehicle where human sit and stand very close together. So close that I learned that some humans have not very nice smells coming from them. A nasty gas comes from their mouths and stinky water trickles from their armpits, and then obviously there is methane. I did not enjoy being on that bus.

My Friend the Alien © Zanib Mian 2020.
Reproduced with the permission of Bloomsbury Publishing Plc

13

FICTION

Then when I went to the park, where some of them were running around (extremely slowly) and some were walking with the little humans. I thought I'd run too, but some of them started looking at me and pointing, so I stopped. At the place I sat down, one human was showing its tiny little dog to another human. I guess it was a baby dog, but I forgot the name for those.

The human was saying, "Awww, isn't he just the most adorable thing?" And her face was changing and she kept putting her hand on her heart.

I felt nothing. It's just a creature. What's the big deal? But I think it might be something to do with the love feeling that his human was suffering from. Then she said," he's so fluffy and cute, I just want to eat him."

So I found out that feelings can happen by looking at things and humans want to eat things they think are cute. I got a bit closer to see how they smell, but the little dog started going crazy and showing me its teeth. It wasn't speaking human, but it was pretty clear it wanted to eat ME. So I ran and it ran after me. It was nowhere near as fast as me, but to be safe, I dropped to the floor and became invisible. The dog ran on, confused.

Sheesh, What just happened there? It seems even the animals here have feelings. I'm not sure I can complete my mission by myself. It's colossal! Also, I haven't heard a squeak out of you guys since I got here. Are you glad to be rid of me?

The activities on these pages are about *My Friend the Alien*.

◯ SIMPLE QUESTIONS

Look at the paragraph beginning...

1 'I ate my first human food today!'

Why do you think the speaker enjoyed the chocolate so much?

_____

2 'Then when I went to the park.'

Why do you think the speaker stopped running when people looked at them?

_____

3 'I guess it was a baby dog.'

How can you tell the speaker doesn't understand humans' love for pets?

_____

4 'The dog ran on, confused.'

Why do you think the speaker dropped to the floor and became invisible?

_____

✪ SENTENCE INFERENCE

1 'The place was full of purple gas, which the humans released as they pushed around these metal cages...'

What are the metal cages that Maxx is talking about?

_____

2 'I learned that some humans have not very nice smells coming from them. A nasty gas comes from their mouths and stinky water trickles from their armpits...'

What are the stinky water trickles? Tick **one**.

tears ☐
saliva ☐
sweat ☐
snot ☐

🧠 THIS SUGGESTS...

'I felt nothing. It's just a creature. What's the big deal?' What does this suggest about the Maxx's view of the small dog? Tick **one**.

Maxx is not interested in the dog. ☐

Maxx finds the dog adorable. ☐

Maxx is scared of the dog. ☐

🔍 EVIDENCE

1 'I did not enjoy being on that bus.'
How can you tell Maxx disliked their experience on the bus?

1 _____

2 _____

2 What impression do you get about how Maxx views human emotions? Give **two** impressions, using evidence from the text to support your answer.

Impression	Evidence

✅ SUMMARY

What best describes Maxx's feelings at the end of the text? Tick **one**.

Maxx feels successful about his journey. ☐

Maxx feels abandoned and lonely. ☐

Maxx feels happy and excited about the future. ☐

THE JUNGLE PERSONIFIED

ANDREW JENNINGS

The mighty drummer pounds upon the earth,
With fists like thunder striking roots and stone,
His broad chest rises, full of quiet strength,
Eyes deep and knowing, watching the wild unfold,
He sits, a king upon his green throne.

The shadowed prowler slips between the leaves,
Silent as breath, yet heavy with intent,
Muscles ripple beneath a coat of dusk,
Golden eyes pierce the undergrowth,
Ready to seize the heartbeat of the earth.

The armoured knight stomps through the green,
Ancient and slow, yet unyielding in his march,
He wears his heavy crown of ivory and time,
Each footfall marks a memory in the soil,
The earth bends to his ancient will.

14

POETRY

The winged dancer twirls in the canopy,
Her feathers flash like forgotten dreams,
She sings in a voice both sweet and wild,
Charming the day with her jewel-bright notes,
A flash of life in the emerald sky.

The silent architect builds with patient hands,
In the quiet hum of industry, she spins her thread,
Her delicate fortress gleams in the light,
A masterpiece of geometry and purpose,
Ready to trap the careless wanderer.

The sly hypnotist slithers through the brush,
His liquid body flows like whispered secrets,
Tongue flickering, tasting the warm breath of prey,
Coiled and poised with ancient patience,
Waiting for the perfect moment to strike.

The activities on these pages are about *The Jungle Personified*.

🕮 SIMPLE QUESTIONS

Look at the paragraph beginning...

1 'The mighty drummer pounds upon the earth.'

How can you tell that the mighty drummer is powerful?

_____

2 'The mighty drummer pounds upon the earth.'

How can you tell that he has authority?

_____

3 'The shadowed prowler slips between the leaves.'

How can you tell that the shadowed prowler is stealthy?

_____

4 'The silent architect.'

How can you tell that her work is dangerous for others?

_____

✪ SENTENCE INFERENCE

1 'Tongue flickering, tasting the warm breath of prey,
Coiled and poised with ancient patience'
What animal is this section referring to?

_____

2 'The silent architect builds with patient hands.'
What animal might this stanza be describing? Tick **one**.

- A spider ☐
- A gorilla ☐
- A bird ☐
- A tiger ☐

🙂 THIS SUGGESTS...

'The armoured knight stomps through the green, ancient and slow, yet unyielding in his march.' What does this suggest about the armoured knight?

He is weak and tired. ☐

He is quick and playful. ☐

He is strong and determined. ☐

🔍 EVIDENCE

1. Look at the stanza beginning: 'The winged dancer twirls in the canopy.' How can you tell that the winged dancer is graceful and vibrant?

   1 _____
   _____

   2 _____
   _____

2. What impression do you get of the armoured knight? Give **two** impressions, using evidence from the text to support your answer.

Impression	Evidence

✅ SUMMARY

How is the 'armoured knight' different from the 'winged dancer'? Tick **one**.

The armoured knight is small, while the winged dancer is large. ☐

The armoured knight flies, while the winged dancer stomps on the ground. ☐

The armoured knight is slow and heavy, while the winged dancer is light and quick. ☐

MISCHIEF ON THE MOORS

STEPHEN DAVIES

The road levelled out at the bottom as it entered Becca Woods. The girls juddered over the cattle grid and across an ancient stone bridge with the brook babbling beneath. As they rounded a corner in the road, they came across an unexpected sight: six woolly-headed alpacas standing in the road.

The gate to the Becky Falls animal sanctuary had been knocked clean off its hinges, and the fence of the alpaca pen lay in splinters on the ground.

Using a plank of wood as a ramp, Libby and Daisy soared over the debris and landed in the field beyond, still pedalling hard. The tyre marks of the mole catcher's car were clear to see, and the girls were hot on his tail. They jumped another shattered fence, and slogged their way uphill through the forest, past limpid pools and tumbling waterfalls.

"Look!" Daisy pointed to the other side of the brook. "Butchart's car has crashed!"

"There are stepping stones ahead!" called Libby. "How are your bunny hops these days?"

"Better than yours," laughed Daisy.

They crossed the stepping stones in a series of rapid jumps, then stood up tall in their saddles and powered up the far bank, which was carpeted with sun-dappled bluebells.

The mole catcher's car had smacked head-on into a silver birch tree. Smoke rose from the crumpled bonnet and the driver's door stood open.

"He's on foot now!" cried Libby. "We've got the advantage!"

They rode up a footpath, through a muddy puddle and out onto open moorland. This area was known as Hound Tor Marshes, and Mum and Dad were always warning them about it. One false step, girls, and you'll disappear into the slurping bog, never to be seen again.

Mr Butchart was right there in front of them, and he had already taken more than one false step. He was sinking further with every movement, yet still he blundered forward.

Libby and Daisy rode up over the bridleway and came down onto a patch of stony ground a few yards from the hapless mole catcher.

"Stop moving!" Libby yelled.

"You're making it worse!"

"Nonsense!" Mr Butchart waved the chuckling pixie high above his head. "I'm on my way to London, where this little fellow will make my fortune!"

Mischief on the Moors © Stephen Davies 2023. Reproduced with the permission of Bloomsbury Publishing Plc

Mischief on the Moors © Stephen Davies 2023.
Reproduced with the permission of Bloomsbury Publishing Plc

"This isn't the way to London!" called Daisy. "You're being pixie led!"

At the words 'pixie led', Mr Butchart seemed to come to his senses. "By Jupiter, you're right!" he said, his cheeks turning suddenly pale. "This imp has proper done me in. Crashed my car, and everything!"

"Take off your jacket, and turn it inside out," said Libby. "It will break the spell."

"I can't do that!" Mr Butchart yelled. "I'm not letting go of the imp!"

The pixie giggled and clapped its tiny hands.

"Mr Butchart, you need to choose!" cried Libby. "Drown with the pixie or survive without it!"

The bog was up to Mr Butchart's waist, sucking and slurping.

"Choose!" screamed Daisy.

Mr Butchart looked down at the bog and his will crumbled in an instant. He put the pixie down on the bog grass, whipped off his jacket and turned it inside-out.

The pixie gave an elaborate bow and scampered off in the direction of Haytor. Daisy could have sworn it gave her a little thumbs-up sign as it sprinted away.

The mole catcher shifted his weight onto his tummy and wriggled across the bog towards the safety of the stony ground. Libby and Daisy grabbed one hand each and pulled him to safety.

"Thank you," gasped the frightened man. "If you two hadn't arrived when you did, I dread to think what might have happened. I was crazy to imagine I could have made my fortune out of that nasty little imp."

The activities on these pages are about *Mischief on the Moors*.

🥷 SIMPLE QUESTIONS

Look at the paragraph beginning...

1 'The gate to the Becky Falls animal sanctuary...'

How can you tell that the alpacas were not supposed to be in the road?

_____

2 'Butchart's car has crashed!'

Why do you think the girls felt they had an advantage after seeing the car?

_____

3 'Stop moving!'

Why did Libby yell at Mr. Butchart to stop moving?

_____

4 'Choose!' screamed Daisy.

How can you tell that Mr. Butchart was scared?

_____

✚ SENTENCE INFERENCE

1 'The pixie gave an elaborate bow and scampered off in the direction of Haytor. Daisy could have sworn it gave her a little thumbs-up sign as it sprinted away.'

What does this passage tell you about the pixie's personality?

_____

2 'This area was known as Hound Tor Marshes, and Mum and Dad were always warning them about it. One false step, girls, and you'll disappear into the slurping bog, never to be seen again.'

This passage reflects a sense of? Tick **one**.

- messiness ☐
- danger ☐
- confusion ☐
- anger ☐

👁 THIS SUGGESTS...

'Stop moving!' Libby yelled. 'You're making it worse!' What does this suggest about Libby's feelings at that moment?

She is frustrated with Mr. Butchart. ☐

She is worried about Mr. Butchart. ☐

She doesn't care about Mr. Butchart. ☐

🔍 EVIDENCE

1 'Mr Butchart was right there in front of them, and he had already taken more than one false step.' How can you tell that Mr. Butchart is in danger?

1 _____

2 _____

2 How can you tell that Libby and Daisy are brave? Give **three** pieces of evidence.

1 _____

2 _____

3 _____

✅ SUMMARY

What best describes the difference between Libby and Mr. Butchart's attitudes toward the pixie? Tick **one**.

Mr. Butchart is scared of the pixie, while Libby admires its mischief. ☐

Both Libby and Mr. Butchart feel tricked by the pixie. ☐

Libby wants to save the pixie, but Mr. Butchart sees it as a way to get rich. ☐

THE LAB BOOK OF MARIE CURIE

ANDREW JENNINGS

9 July, 1898

Today was a remarkable day! I isolated a new element from uranium ore. I can hardly believe it: this element glows with a strange light, and I can feel the excitement buzzing in the air of my lab. I wonder if others will see the marvels that I see. Perhaps this discovery will change the world. But it's heavy work, and the air is thick with dust from the ore. I have to be careful; it's not just a game of discovery.

20 July, 1898

I've named the new element 'polonium' after my beloved homeland, Poland. As I write this, I can still feel the weight of my decision. It's as if I've given a piece of my heart to this work. I watch as the polonium gives off energy, like the warmth of the sun on a cool day. I wonder how people will react when they learn about this. Will they understand its importance?

7 November, 1898

Today was challenging. I spent hours in the lab, working with my husband, Pierre. We both feel the heat of our passion for science. Our hands are often stained with the remnants of our experiments, and our clothes are dusty. But I cherish these moments. They remind me of why I do this work. We are on the brink of something great.

15 January, 1899

I feel tired, but my excitement pushes me forward. I've discovered that polonium is radioactive! It's as if the element has its own pulse, a heartbeat of its own. I must keep this a secret for now. The world might not be ready for this news, but I know it's important. If only I could share it with the children in my hometown. I want them to know that they can be curious about the world around them.

FICTIONAL DIARY ENTRY

23 April, 1902

Today, I finally succeeded in isolating another new element: radium! The very name brings a sense of brightness. It's energetic, almost like it wants to leap off the table! But I am cautious. There's a weight to this discovery that feels different. I've read that this element could help to heal many people. But I must remind myself to be careful. My hands have developed small burns from handling these materials. It's a reminder that great discoveries come with risks.

10 December, 1903

I received wonderful news today! Pierre and I are awarded the Nobel Prize in Physics along with Henri Becquerel for our work on radioactivity. I can hardly believe it! This prize is not just for me; it's for all women in science. I wonder how many doors this will open for future generations. I can already see the spark of hope in the eyes of young girls who dream of becoming a scientist like me.

26 May, 1906

Tragedy struck today. Pierre was taken from me in an accident, and I'm lost without him. He was my partner in every sense. I will carry on our work, but my heart is heavy. I write this entry through tears, remembering his laughter and our shared dreams. I know he would want me to keep pushing forward, so I will.

10 December, 1911

After much hard work, I've received a second Nobel Prize, this time in Chemistry, for my discoveries of radium and polonium. It feels surreal. I am filled with a mix of pride and sorrow. I can't help but wonder: What will my discoveries lead to? Will they change the lives of many, or will they remain hidden in the shadows?

16 THE LAB BOOK OF MARIE CURIE

The activities on these pages are about *The Lab Book of Marie Curie*.

SIMPLE QUESTIONS

Look at the paragraph beginning...

1 Look at the entry dated '9 July, 1898'.

How can you tell that Marie Curie feels excited about her discovery?

_____

2 Look at the entry dated '7 November, 1898'.

How do you know that Marie enjoys working with her husband, Pierre?

_____

3 Look at the entry dated '23 April, 1902'.

How can you tell that Marie is cautious about handling radium?

_____

4 Look at the entry dated '26 May, 1906'.

How do you know that Marie is deeply affected by Pierre's death?

_____

SENTENCE INFERENCE

1 'I am filled with a mix of pride and sorrow.'

Why do you think that Marie Curie is filled with sorrow?

_____

2 'But it's heavy work, and the air is thick with dust from the ore. I have to be careful; it's not just a game of discovery.'

In this passage, what sense do you get of the work? A sense of…Tick **one**.

- mystery ☐
- history ☐
- pride ☐
- danger ☐

🌐 THIS SUGGESTS...

'I can hardly believe it, this element glows with a strange light.'
What does this suggest about Marie's discovery? Tick **one**.

It is quite ordinary. ☐

It is unusual and fascinating. ☐

It seems important. ☐

🔍 EVIDENCE

1. Look at the entry dated '9 July, 1898'. How can you tell that Marie Curie is excited about her discovery? Give **two** ways.

   1 _____
   _____

   2 _____
   _____

2. What impression do you get of Marie Curie's resilience in the face of challenges? Give **two** impressions, using evidence from the text to support your answer.

Impression	Evidence

✅ SUMMARY

What kind of person do you think Marie Curie was?

A relaxed and carefree person who avoids hard work. ☐

Someone who is only interested in fame and awards. ☐

A dedicated scientist who perseveres through challenges. ☐

MARK OF THE CYCLOPS

SAVIOUR PIROTTA

The Temple on the Hill

'That was a very eventful journey,' said Thrax after we'd stabled Ariana and were exploring Zenon's house. 'Sailors quarrelling over mice. Pirates chasing us across the sea. Bandits in the wilderness. The gruesome death of a trusted slave. You should write it all down, Nico, so we can read about it when we're old and our memories start to fade.'

I blinked at him in surprise. 'How do you mean?'

'I noticed you are very good with words,' replied Thrax. 'You should be doing something more interesting with your skills than taking down Master Ariston's rubbish.'

It had never occurred to me to write anything except what Master Ariston dictated but, now that Thrax had put the idea in my head, I was quite taken by it. All the people I admired were writers: playwrights, poets, historians... perhaps I too could become one of them.

But what sort of writing would I do? Sappho the poet was famous for her volumes of romantic lyrics, Herodotus for his fanciful accounts of historical events and famous people, Homer for epics that retold ancient myths. I needed to find a genre of writing that best suited my talents.

'Look at this kitchen,' said Thrax, interrupting my thoughts. 'It's got the biggest bread oven I've ever seen.'

Although the slaves' quarters in Master Zenon's house were cramped, the rest of the building was palatial. It had at least ten rooms that I could count, including a large hall – the andron – where Master Zenon entertained his friends. The women had a similar space – the gynaikeion – upstairs, where they spent most of the day spinning, weaving or sharing meals with close friends and relatives.

Behind the house was a narrow lane leading to a small farm and an orchard where Master Zenon's slaves grew vegetables, tended fruit trees and kept sheep and goats for milk. Here also were the stables where we'd left Ariana and a dovecote so lavish it looked like a small temple.

Master Ariston was given an airy room next to Master Zenon's, which he considered a great honour. He was quite impressed with the décor of the house, which was much grander and more colourful than we were used to in Athens.

'Father would call the style vulgar,' he said as we set out to explore Corinth the next morning.

Mark of the Cyclops: An Ancient Greek Mystery © Saviour Pirotta 2017.
Reproduced with the permission of Bloomsbury Publishing Plc

17

FICTION

'But I think it quite takes the breath away. You should see the bathroom, Nico. Such a huge bath, you can practically swim in it. And the mosaics! There are mermaids and water nymphs all over the walls.'

Thrax and I had in fact already seen the bathroom. We had sneaked in during the night and cheekily given ourselves a good long wash and a rub down with perfumed oil. Rich masters might think slaves and badly paid scribes are not capable of appreciating the finer things in life but we are. It's just not in our interest to let them know about it.

Corinth was a bigger city than Athens, with smellier roads and much louder people. It had several temples, public baths, a theatre and the agora we'd seen the night before. These all lay in the shadow of the Acropolis high on the hill. Master Ariston told us locals called it the Acrocorinth. It had a famous temple of Aphrodite, whose beautiful priestesses were said to attract sailors from all over Hellas. Close to the temple was a sacred spring, which gushed out of the rocks into a large bathhouse. Legend told that Pegasus had created it by striking the bare rocks with his hooves.

'One hour in its pools is believed to give authors enough inspiration for a month,' Master Ariston informed us. 'I wish we had a magic spring like it back in Athens. I would bathe in it every day and write the most admired poems in the world.'

The city also had a paved road that led to a busy harbour. Here a weary traveller or sailor could revive himself drinking in one of the taverns that gave Corinth its reputation as the liveliest capital in the world.

Master Ariston dragged us up the hill to the Acrocorinth, as he wanted to bathe in the sacred spring at once. We were not the only people there taking the waters. A rather sickly-looking man with straggly hair and blotchy skin was sitting in one of the pools, his long curly beard moving lazily with the current.

'I'm Euripides,' he introduced himself. Master Ariston leaned forward, his wet nostrils flaring with excitement. 'THE Euripides?'

'I am a well-known writer of tragedies,' confirmed the man.

The activities on these pages are about *Mark of the Cyclops*.

🥷 SIMPLE QUESTIONS

Look at the paragraph beginning...

1 'That was a very eventful journey,' said Thrax...'

How can you tell that Thrax found the journey memorable?

_____

2 'Corinth was a bigger city than Athens...'

How can you tell Corinth is a lively and busy city?

_____

3 'Thrax and I had in fact already seen the bathroom...'

How do you know Thrax and Nico secretly enjoyed the luxuries in the house?

_____

4 'One hour in its pools is believed to give authors enough inspiration...'

Why do you think Master Ariston is eager to bathe in the sacred spring?

_____

✥ SENTENCE INFERENCE

1 'We were not the only people there taking the waters. A rather sickly-looking man with straggly hair and blotchy skin was sitting in one of the pools, his long curly beard moving lazily with the current.'

How would you describe the man's age?

_____

2 'Although the slaves' quarters in Master Zenon's house were cramped, the rest of the building was palatial.'

What does this sentence tell you about Master Zenon's house? It was like a... Tick **one**.

harbour ☐
mansion ☐
palace ☐
villa ☐

THIS SUGGESTS...

'It had at least ten rooms that I could count, including a large hall – the andron – where Master Zenon entertained his friends.' What does this suggest about Master Zenon's lifestyle? Tick **one**.

He dislikes having visitors. ☐

He doesn't care about luxury. ☐

He is wealthy and enjoys hosting. ☐

EVIDENCE

1. 'Thrax and I had in fact already seen the bathroom…' How can you tell that Thrax and Nico enjoyed sneaking into the bathroom? Give **two** ways.

    1 _____

    _____

    2 _____

    _____

2. What impression do you get of the city of Corinth? Give two impressions, using evidence from the text to support your answer.

Impression	Evidence

SUMMARY

What best describes how Master Ariston feels about the house in Corinth? Tick **one**.

He thinks it is too big and grand. ☐

He finds it beautiful and impressive. ☐

He feels it is messy and unorganised. ☐

THE BOY WHO GREW A TREE

POLLY HO-YEN

Nature-loving Timi is unsettled by the arrival of a new sibling and starts caring for a tree growing in his local library. There is something magical about the tree…

Chapter 10

The library was still standing, Timi noticed with relief, when he first managed to get away from his cousins.

His mum had been wrong about them spending more time together now, and wrong about Bisi wanting to talk to him. He still went to the after-school club and spent a few nights every week with his auntie who lived close by.

The only good thing about this was that it was easy to slip away from his cousins again.

The door of the library felt a little stiffer than it had before. Timi had to lean his weight against it to open it. When he was inside, there was a moment when he was sure that the tree wasn't there but, as he walked into the main room, he saw that it was, and was as tall as it was when he'd last visited, although no bigger.

It was still standing but it looked grey. Its leaves were dull and they drooped on the branches. One strong gust of wind might whip them from the tree for good. The trunk looked almost sagging, leaning to one side ever so slightly as though it were tired.

'I'm sorry, I'm sorry,' Timi whispered to the tree urgently as he tipped a bucket of water into the crack. He hoped that the tree might start to look better immediately but it continued to look withered and weak. It didn't even seem to Timi like it was talking back to him anymore, but he spoke to it anyway.

"Do you need more?" he asked it.

He filled the bucket again and gave it another long drink. Then he went to the window on the other side of the library that was not by the road, so people wouldn't be able to look in, and pull the curtain open a bit more, so more light fell onto its branches. The curtain was stuck at first but Timi tugged at it until he managed to pull it open wide.

The sun's rays filled the room and when Timi looked back at the tree he thought that it already looked a little bit greener than it had when he first came in.

"Are you feeling better?" Timi asked the tree. "Have you had enough to drink?"

The way he'd always been able to tell with one of his pots in his little garden if they'd had enough water, was by feeling the soil to see if it felt damp and looked black with moisture. But here in the library, he couldn't see any soil, just the criss-cross of the floorboards.

He laid his hands against the floorboards at the base of the trunk. They felt damp from the last bucket of water and so Timi trusted that the tree had had enough. Also, he promised himself, he would be back tomorrow to check on it.

Chapter 11

The next day when Timi returned to the library, the tree had grown a full metre overnight. Timi could no longer even touch the top of it.

He only had a little bit of time before he was due back at his auntie's for dinner, so he spent most of his time in the library lugging buckets of water from the kitchen to the tree, until he felt satisfied that the tree had had enough to drink.

"I'll come back again soon," he told it before he left. He felt calmer seeing that the tree had not only grown but looked as healthy as it did before the holidays when he had gone away.

The activities on these pages are about *The Boy Who Grew a Tree*.

✦ SIMPLE QUESTIONS

Look at the paragraph beginning…

1 'The door of the library felt a little stiffer…'

Why do you think Timi had to push hard to open the door?

_____

2 'Its leaves were dull…'

How can you tell that the tree was struggling?

_____

3 'The sun's rays…'

Why do you think Timi opened the curtain wider?

_____

4 'The next day when Timi returned to the library…'

How can you tell the tree had recovered?

_____

✦ SENTENCE INFERENCE

1 'The only good thing about this was that it was easy to slip away from his cousins again.'

What does this tell us about Timi's relationship with his cousins?

_____

2 'I'm sorry, I'm sorry,' Timi whispered to the tree urgently.'

How does Timi feel about the sagging tree? A sense of… Tick **one**.

- relief ☐
- pride ☐
- responsibility ☐
- jealousy ☐

🌳 THIS SUGGESTS...

'The tree looked grey, its leaves drooped, and the trunk leaned slightly...'
What does this suggest about the tree? Tick **one**.

The tree is struggling to survive. ☐

The tree is strong and healthy. ☐

The tree doesn't need help. ☐

🔍 EVIDENCE

1. 'The next day when Timi returned to the library...'
   How can you tell that the tree is magical?

   1 _____

   2 _____

2. 'Timi laid his hands against the floorboards.'
   How can you tell that Timi is determined to care for the tree?

   1 _____

   2 _____

✅ SUMMARY

What best describes Timi's attitude toward the library? Tick **one**.

Timi avoids spending time at the library. ☐

Timi thinks the library is only for adults. ☐

Timi sees the library as a magical and special place. ☐

PING AND THE MISSING RING

EMMA SHEVAH

Chapter 1 – Half Term

Finally, the day had arrived. As Ping packed her suitcase, she was so excited she could barely speak. If she did, the words might burst from her mouth in a blast of heat, noise and energy, and that would not do at all. Not in Ping's family. You see, Ping and her family were Thai, and the custom for Thai people is to be calm, composed and polite. Typically, Thai people do not appreciate words bursting in blasts from people's mouths – even eager, excited words. Certainly not cross, cantankerous ones – that was not acceptable in the least. Whenever Ping spoke too quickly or too loudly, or when her tone turned as dark as a country road at night, her parents would frown a little and murmur, "Shh, shh, Ping. Please be calm, OK?"

Ping tried – she really did – but being calm was difficult. She seemed to have springs in her shoes, bubbles in her body, and roars and giggles and yells trying to leap free from her lungs to the tips of the trees. When she felt the bubbles rise and the giggles gather, she would firmly clamp a lid on top, but all too often it would rip off when she least expected it and whatever was inside her would explode outwards noisily. Now she was excited about the visit, it was almost impossible to keep the lid on.

"How are you getting on?" Ping's mother asked her, drifting to Ping's bedroom door, her dark hair secured in a neat bun at the nape of her neck. Ping's mother, Chabah, seemed to glide rather than walk, as if she were a weightless cloud wafting over a warm current of air. She had once been a classical Thai dancer, and now she taught dance to students near their home. She moved elegantly and gracefully as if she were always performing a slow flowing dance to a mesmerised audience, but it was simply the dance of her life: the dance of slotting bills in her business folders, the dance of folding the laundry, the dance of paying for parcels at the Post Office. Ping liked how she moved her hands most of all. Even the way her mother washed an apple was poetic, gentle and unhurried, as though she were bathing, with the tenderest love and care, the head of a new born baby.

Ping and the Missing Ring © Emma Shevah 2021.
Reproduced with the permission of Bloomsbury Publishing Plc

19

FICTION

Ping was getting on fine, in fact, so she nodded to keep the lid on. Her mother had already placed her clothes in a pile on the chair – all Ping needed to do was pack them. But then she just had to speak. "You were the last one to use the case!" she cried, almost erupting with delight at her genius detective work. She'd found a lone long black hair lying across the shell of the empty suitcase, and a single white trainer sock, unworn, in the zip pocket. In truth, it hadn't been difficult to work out – her mother had returned from a trip a few days ago and Ping had known she taken that particular suitcase because she'd seen it in the back of the car – but that didn't bother Ping. She was perfecting her powers of perception and honing her noticing skills, and she was definitely, definitely getting better.

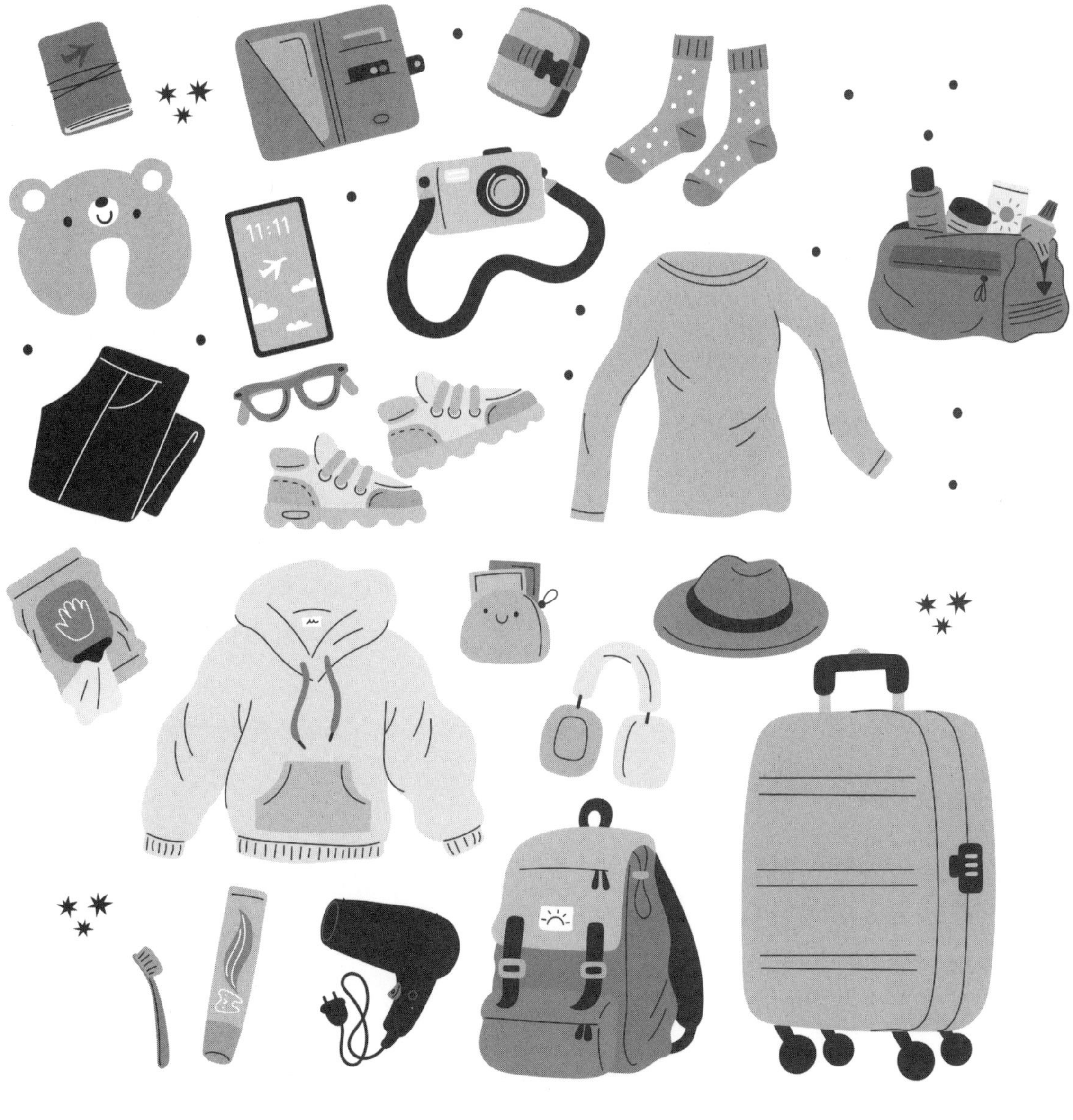

The activities on these pages are about *Ping and the Missing Ring*.

🥷 SIMPLE QUESTIONS

Look at the paragraph beginning…

1 'Finally, the day had arrived.'

How can you tell Ping is excited about her trip?

_____

2 'Ping tried – she really did.'

How can you tell that Ping finds it hard to stay calm?

_____

3 'Her mother had already placed her clothes.'

How can you tell that Ping's mother helps her stay organised?

_____

4 'You were the last one to use the case!'

How can you tell that Ping enjoys solving small mysteries?

_____

✳ SENTENCE INFERENCE

1 'She seemed to have springs in her shoes, bubbles in her body, and roars and giggles and yells trying to leap free from her lungs.'

What do you think the phrase **'springs in her shoes'** means?

_____

2 'Even the way her mother washed an apple was poetic, gentle and unhurried, as though she were bathing, with the tenderest love and care, the head of a new born baby.'

What sense does this give you about Ping's mother? A sense of…Tick **one**.

love ☐
caring ☐
anger ☐
beauty ☐

🗨 THIS SUGGESTS...

'Her mother seemed to glide rather than walk, as if she were a weightless cloud wafting over a warm current of air.'
What does this suggest about Ping's mother? Tick **one**.

She is graceful and elegant. ☐

She is clumsy and hurried. ☐

She is always in a rush. ☐

🔍 EVIDENCE

1 'Ping seemed to have springs in her shoes.'
How can you tell that Ping finds it difficult to stay calm?

1 _____

2 _____

2 What impression do you get of how Ping feels about her mother?
Give **two** impressions, using evidence from the text to support your answer.

Impression	Evidence

✅ SUMMARY

What best describes Ping's relationship with her mother? Tick **one**.

Ping feels that her mother is too strict. ☐

Ping admires her mother's grace and calmness. ☐

Ping thinks her mother doesn't understand her. ☐

ROAD TRIP USA: EXPLORING AMERICA'S WONDERS

ANDREW JENNINGS

The United States is a vast country full of incredible places to explore. A road trip across the USA takes you through different landscapes and cultures. From towering mountains to endless deserts, from bustling cities to quiet towns, there's something for everyone on a road trip across America!

The Famous Route 66

One of the most famous road trips in America is along Route 66. This historic highway stretches over 2,000 miles, connecting Chicago in the Midwest to Los Angeles on the West Coast. Sometimes called the 'Main Street of America', Route 66 passes through eight states: Illinois, Missouri, Kansas, Oklahoma, Texas, New Mexico, Arizona and California.

As you drive down Route 66, you'll see classic roadside diners, quirky motels and neon signs that light up the night. Many people travel this road to experience a slice of old America. You can even spot giant statues and unusual roadside attractions like the Cadillac Ranch, where cars are buried nose-down in the ground, or the world's largest rocking chair in Missouri!

Stunning National Parks

Another must-see on a road trip across the USA are the national parks. These parks are home to some of the most beautiful natural wonders in the world. From the towering peaks of Yosemite National Park in California to the deep canyons of Grand Canyon National Park in Arizona, each park offers something unique.

At the Grand Canyon, you can stand on the edge of one of the world's largest and deepest canyons. The view stretches for miles, with red and orange rocks glowing in the sunlight. It's a sight that takes your breath away! If you're lucky, you might even see a bald eagle soaring high above.

In Yellowstone National Park, located in Wyoming, Montana and Idaho, you can witness geysers shoot boiling water into the air. The most famous geyser, Old Faithful, erupts every 90 minutes, shooting water as high as 55 metres! Yellowstone is also home to bison, elk and even bears. Driving through these wild landscapes, you get a sense of how large and diverse America's wilderness is.

Adventures

Not all road trips are about nature! The USA is also home to vibrant cities that are perfect for a visit. In the East, the Statue of Liberty welcomes visitors to New York City, where towering skyscrapers, famous landmarks like Central Park and bustling streets full of yellow taxis await.

20

NON-FICTION

As you drive down the East Coast, you might stop in Washington, D.C., the capital city. Here, you can visit important sites like the White House and the Lincoln Memorial, where huge statues and buildings tell the story of America's history.

On the West Coast, you'll find the city of San Francisco, where the Golden Gate Bridge stretches across the bay. You might even take a trolley ride up and down the city's steep streets! And don't forget Hollywood in Los Angeles, where you might spot a celebrity or two on the famous Walk of Fame.

The Open Road

One of the best parts of a road trip is the freedom it gives you. The open road stretches out before you and with every mile, there's a new adventure waiting. You can stop whenever you want to see a new sight or try a local food you've never had before. In the southern state of Louisiana, you might taste spicy Cajun food, while in Texas, it's all about barbecues!

The road trip also teaches patience. Driving for hours can be tiring, but the reward is the chance to see so many different parts of the country. Whether you're passing through the rolling green hills of Virginia or the endless deserts of Nevada, the changing landscapes show just how big and varied the USA is.

Road Trip Fun

Road trips aren't just about where you're going – they're also about how you get there. Families and friends often bring snacks, music and games to play along the way. Some people love counting how many different state licence plates they see, while others look for wildlife or interesting sights out of the window. The road becomes an adventure in itself!

The activities on these pages are about *Road Trip USA: Exploring America's Wonders.*

🥷 SIMPLE QUESTIONS

Look at the paragraph beginning...

1 'The Famous Route 66.'

How can you tell that Route 66 is special to people who travel on it?

_____

2 'The United States is a vast country.'

How can you tell that travelling across the USA would show many different types of places?

_____

3 'Stunning National Parks.'

How do you know that national parks are popular stops for travellers?

_____

4 'In Yellowstone National Park.'

How do you know that Yellowstone has features you might not find elsewhere?

_____

✥ SENTENCE INFERENCE

1 'Not all road trips are about nature! The USA is also home to vibrant cities that are perfect for a visit…'

What does the word **'vibrant'** tell us about the cities on Route 66?

_____

2 'At the Grand Canyon, you can stand on the edge of one of the world's largest and deepest canyons. The view stretches for miles.'

Standing at the Grand Canyon, what might visitors feel a sense of? Tick **one**.

- fear ☐
- happiness ☐
- gratefulness ☐
- awe ☐

🚗 THIS SUGGESTS...

'The view stretches for miles, with red and orange rocks glowing in the sunlight.'

What does this suggest about the landscape of the Grand Canyon? Tick **one**.

It is dark and gloomy. ☐

It is crowded with people. ☐

It is vast and impressive. ☐

🔍 EVIDENCE

1 How can you tell that the Grand Canyon is an impressive sight? Give **two** ways.

1 _____

2 _____

2 What impression do you get of Route 66? Give **two** impressions, using evidence from the text to support your answer.

Impression	Evidence

✅ SUMMARY

What is the main reason people enjoy traveling on Route 66? Tick **one**.

They want to reach their destination quickly. ☐

They prefer the quiet and peaceful atmosphere. ☐

They enjoy the unique and historic sights along the way. ☐

Answers are provided below, with the / sign indicating multiple options, but marks may be awarded for any other logical inference not mentioned (with supporting evidence if required).

1. BELLA'S DEN
SIMPLE QUESTIONS
1. They had to sit crouched together / There wasn't room to lie down.
2. The moonlight made the surroundings look as bright as day.
3. The holes are described as deep and black, making them seem strange.
4. It was watching them carefully / trying to figure out if they were a threat.
5. The narrator said their skin was 'ice cold' and they felt 'frozen with fear.' / The narrator not daring to move or breathe.
6. The first fox's actions signalled that it was safe for the others to come out.
7. They were rolling, jumping and playing games like little children.
8. The narrator feels that nothing else in the world is as important as the foxes playing.
9. She turned her head sharply / she led the cubs back into the hole.
10. Because it was so dark once the moon had disappeared.

SENTENCE INFERENCE
1. The narrator touches Bella's arm instead of speaking / Bella answers with a little breath instead of talking.
2. wonder
3. They moved quickly / in a rush / awkwardly.
4. wary
5. The cubs are hitting each other playfully.

THIS SUGGESTS...
1. The narrator feels scared.
2. The fox feels safe.
3. It feels magical and special.
4. She moves quickly and smoothly.

EVIDENCE – TWO MARKS
1. The narrator says they didn't dare move or breathe. // The narrator describes their skin as ice-cold and frozen with fear.
1. The fox relaxes. // The fox turns its head, signalling that it feels at ease. // The cubs start playing and tumbling around, showing no fear.
2. The cubs jump on each other and roll down to the river. // The narrator hears the little puffs of sound they make when they play.
3. The narrator says, 'I'm not sure if I really saw it or not.' // The narrator describes the final shape as a 'dark flutter' suggesting uncertainty.

EVIDENCE – THREE MARKS
1. The narrator describes the fox cubs playing as if it were the 'middle of the world.' // The narrator feels that nothing else in the world is as important. // They hold their breath and feel frozen while watching the foxes, showing how captivated they are. // The narrator compares the vixen's movement to water, highlighting how graceful and magical the scene felt.
2. **Calm:** The narrator describes the night as a 'black curtain' that is peaceful and quiet. // **Curious:** The narrator keeps watching the den and notices every little movement, like the fox appearing.
3. **Playful:** The fox cubs jump and roll around like 'kids in a school playground.' // **Energetic:** The cubs run, jump and biff each other, showing they are full of energy. // Obedient/wary: As soon as the vixen senses danger, they immediately go back inside the den.

SUMMARISE
1. Bella sees it as a secret and special place.
2. The narrator feels awe at the magical moment.

SEQUENCE
3. 3, 2, 1, 4

PREDICTION
4. Bella and the narrator will decide to visit the den again another night.

2. THE SCOTS AND THE PICTS
SIMPLE QUESTIONS
1. Dal Riata was on the coast, making it easy to reach by boat.
2. They painted or tattooed their bodies with designs.
3. They were able to establish kingdoms and make alliances.
4. The Picts built strong hillforts.
5. They needed to be stronger to defend against the Vikings.
6. He united the Scots and Picts.
7. They worshipped gods connected to nature / They farmed and raised animals.
8. Because they built monasteries.
9. They left behind their stone carvings.
10. They brought new language, religion, history and culture to Scotland.

SENTENCE INFERENCE
1. water (sea or lake also accepted)
2. worked together
3. originally from Ireland
4. religion
5. They joined forces / worked together

THIS SUGGESTS...
1. The Scots had a lot of influence.
2. The Picts valued and wanted to protect their land.
3. They realised they were stronger together.
4. They had unique and artistic traditions.

EVIDENCE – TWO MARKS

1. They sailed across the sea from Ireland to settle in Scotland. // They established new kingdoms and expanded their influence.
2. They tattooed or painted their bodies. // Their designs were intricate.
3. They built strong hillforts to defend against invaders. // They resisted the Romans, who found them difficult to conquer.
4. They were often in conflict battling for land.// The Vikings began raiding the coasts.

EVIDENCE – THREE MARKS

1. They sailed from Ireland to settle in Scotland. // They established kingdoms. // They made alliances with other tribes. // They spread Christianity across Scotland.
2. **Protective**: The Picts built strong hillforts to defend their land from invaders like the Romans. // **Fierce**: They were known as fierce warriors who lived in northern and eastern Scotland.
3. **Ambitious**: The Scots quickly became powerful, establishing kingdoms and making alliances with other tribes. // **Determined**: They expanded their influence and mingled with local peoples, leaving a lasting mark on Scotland's history.

SUMMARISE

1. They joined together to fight the Vikings.
2. The Picts stayed strong but later joined with the Scots.

SEQUENCE

3. 4, 2, 3, 1

PREDICTION

4. The Vikings might have taken over more land in Scotland.

3. THE GREAT FOODBANK HEIST

SIMPLE QUESTIONS

1. The narrator says they hate those months. / The months are always hard. / The games don't feel fun. / The family are extremely hungry.
2. Because they helped them forget about the food they didn't like.
3. They say it's their favourite game. / They get to choose the weirdest ingredients and wear a real chef's hat.
4. Because the hat is real.
5. Her menus are the prettiest. / They are so special Mum puts them on the fridge.
6. Because it was hard to imagine bad food as something delicious.
7. To help them cope with the food they didn't like by using their imagination.
8. They didn't have enough food to play the games properly. / Thinking about food all the time made them tired.
9. They felt tired so they couldn't use their imaginations as well as usual.
10. The narrator heard her crying at night when she thought no one could hear her.

SENTENCE INFERENCE

1. It tasted weird / disgusting / unusual.
2. pride
3. It was very hot / melted down the sides.
4. She is sad.
5. He doesn't like it.

THIS SUGGESTS...

1. She is creative.
2. They find it fun.
3. She is creative.
4. They are struggling.

EVIDENCE – TWO MARKS

1. She invented creative games like Master Chef and Transformers Game. / She encouraged them to use their imagination, like transforming unpleasant food into something delicious.
2. The narrator got to choose unusual ingredients, like tuna and jam pie. / They wore a real chef's hat with pride while playing the game.
3. She loves drawing and colouring in. / She drew the prettiest designs, like mushrooms with wings and fish with fingers. / Her menus were so special that Mum stuck some on the fridge.
4. They were so hungry that they couldn't sleep. / They sometimes cried at night. / Even Mum cried.

EVIDENCE – THREE MARKS

1. She invented creative games like Master Chef and Transformers Game to make meals more enjoyable. // She pretended to enjoy the games, even when they were difficult, to keep her children positive. // She praised their efforts, like sticking Ashley's special menus on the fridge.
2. **Caring**: Mum created games like Master Chef to make meals more enjoyable and fun for her children. // **Encouraging**: Mum praised Ashley's menus by sticking the special ones on the fridge.
3. **Proud**: The narrator loved inventing dishes like Pineapple Surprise and felt famous for their creativity. // **Frustrated**: During Little Troopers Month, the narrator found it hard to make menus or play games when there wasn't enough food.

SUMMARISE

1. The narrator admires Mum for trying to make things better for them.
2. Mum stays positive by creating games to make meals more enjoyable.

SEQUENCE

3. 3, 2, 4, 1

PREDICTION

4. He will imagine his least favourite food as something amazing.

4. THE STONE AGE TIMES

SIMPLE QUESTIONS

1. It 'sent shockwaves' through the community.
2. It made the food softer and easier to eat.
3. He described it as 'crispy on the outside but soft in the middle.'
4. Thag said people could stay cozy without needing extra furs.
5. Thag said the wolves ran away when they saw the fire.
6. They were tired of cold nights and raw food.
7. She warned that fire is dangerous and mentioned Thag had burned his loincloth.
8. He was thinking about moving it around and making it bigger or smaller.
9. They had ideas for controlling fire and making portable fires.
10. Heating rocks could make new shapes, which would help make tools.

SENTENCE INFERENCE

1. old
2. surprise
3. excited
4. comfortable
5. Move it / take it with them.

THIS SUGGESTS...

1. Thag found fire accidentally.
2. Thag thought it was too hard to eat.
3. Fire scares animals away.
4. Oog is glad to have fire.

EVIDENCE – TWO MARKS

1. Thag didn't expect the spark to appear. // He thought he had angered the gods.
2. Thag said the meat was crispy outside and soft inside. // He said it was easier to eat than raw meat.
3. Oog likes the warmth fire brings. // He is tired of cold nights and raw food.
4. Bora mentions Thag burning his clothes. // She warns that fire needs to be used carefully.

EVIDENCE – THREE MARKS

1. Bora says fire is dangerous // She mentions Thag burned a hole in his loincloth // She warns that they should be careful with fire.
2. **Proud**: Thag describes fire as a 'game-changer' and talks about how it could make life easier. // **Excited or Happy**: Thag explains how cooking meat on fire makes it 'crispy on the outside but soft in the middle,' showing his enthusiasm for this new experience.
3. **Worried**: Bora says, 'we need to be careful,' showing she is concerned about the dangers of fire. // **Scared**: Evidence: Bora mentions Thag 'already burned a hole in his own loincloth,' indicating she is fearful of accidents happening with fire.

SUMMARISE

1. The tribe is excited but also cautious about fire.
2. Thag is excited about the new uses of fire, while Bora is cautious about its dangers.

SEQUENCE

3. 1, 4, 3, 2

PREDICTION

4. They will spend more time around the fire, building a stronger sense of community.

5. AVA'S GONE AND PETS IN CLASS

SIMPLE QUESTIONS

1. Because their best friend, Ava, has been gone for a long time.
2. The teacher might not know when Ava will return. / The teacher doesn't want to upset the narrator.
3. They describe their feelings as heavy and overwhelming.
4. Because Ava isn't there to play with them.
5. They feel as though their world is incomplete without her. / They keep asking and wondering where Ava is.
6. Because it damaged important items like books.
7. Because it caused chaos everywhere it ran.
8. It knocked the chair over.
9. Because the ferrets had a fight.
10. Because the lesson was online. / The pets were not in the teacher's room.

SENTENCE INFERENCE

1. They miss her.
2. The narrator's feelings are strong / They feel very sad, not just a bit.
3. chewed them (a lot)
4. relief
5. They're surprised by the pug.

THIS SUGGESTS...

1. The narrator is hopeful.
2. They feel lonely.
3. The rat is talented and can jump.
4. The Dalmatian is destructive.

EVIDENCE – TWO MARKS

1. The narrator mentions a 'hole' where their friend used to be. // Their best friend has been gone a while. // They keep asking where their friend is. // The halls and playground feel empty without their friend.
2. The narrator has been told Ava will be gone a while. // The teacher doesn't want to answer the question.
3. It wasn't funny. // We got some awkward looks. // They say the class didn't go well.
4. Any mention of an example of the destruction a pet caused. // The narrator says it 'didn't go too well' // calls it 'misrule'.

EVIDENCE – THREE MARKS

1. Bunny - gnawed books // pug - attacked rug // Dalmation - 'dealt damnation' // Hare - knocked over a chair / smashed ornaments // rat - jumped to grab a light // ferrets - had a fight.
2. **A good friend:** narrator calls her their 'best friend' / misses her a lot. **Happy / fun:** the narrator particularly remembers Ava's smile.
3. **Out of control / naughty:** any relevant example. // **Hungry:** the bunny gnaws books. // **Violent:** pug attacks rug / ferrets fight. // **Agile:** rat leaps for light.

SUMMARISE

1. The pets caused chaos, but the teacher was relieved.
2. The narrator feels lonely and misses Ava deeply.

SEQUENCE

3. 1, 3, 4, 2

PREDICTION

4. The teacher announces that Ava has gone away permanently.

6. KID NORMAL

SIMPLE QUESTIONS

1. The weather is horrible.
2. Angry or frustrated.
3. He looks like he's enjoying himself enormously.
4. Because he is too loud in the library.
5. Because Mrs Fletcher looks angry.
6. He feels disappointed.
7. Because he can hear them breathing.
8. Because Mr Flash was rude to her / he said it was too quiet in the library.
9. The people in the library were shocked.
10. Because Mrs Fletcher wants people to be quiet, like a mouse.

SENTENCE INFERENCE

1. Because she's making shushing noises that sound like a kettle steaming.
2. worried
3. She wants people to follow the rules / what she says. // She is not scared of Mr Flash.
4. Murph is confused or unenthusiastic about working with the caretaker.
5. He felt surprised.

THIS SUGGESTS...

1. She wants the library to stay quiet.
2. She gets very angry when someone is noisy.
3. He thinks Murph disrupts the lessons.
4. He likes the idea of punishing Murph.

EVIDENCE – TWO MARKS

1. He ignores her request to 'shh' and speaks again. // He doesn't try to be quiet but speaks in a very loud whisper.
2. He 'barks' at Murph, ie he speaks to him aggressively. // He is angry.
3. He says 'there's not much point you being in my lessons.' // He says: 'Leave the rest of us to get on with some work.' // He is angry and aggressive towards Murph.
4. At first, Murph thinks he will be spending the time out of lessons in the library. // Murph blankly asks, 'The caretaker?' in confusion, showing he's unsure about the situation.

EVIDENCE – THREE MARKS

1. He shouts loudly in the library, even when asked to be quiet. // He calls Mrs Fletcher 'Mrs Mouse' and is rude to her. // He enjoys telling Murph he has to work with the caretaker instead of being in class. // He behaves aggressively.
2. **Nervous:** Sliding down behind his chair. **He doesn't like getting in trouble:** 'Oh noooo.'
3. **Strict:** 'This is a library and I said shush!' // **Bad-tempered:** 'Mrs Fletcher lost her temper.'

SUMMARISE

1. nervous and worried
2. It's a place for silent reading.

SEQUENCE

3. 2, 4, 1, 3

PREDICTION

4. Murph will make a big mess and get in trouble with Mr Flash again.

7. WILDSMITH: INTO THE DARK FOREST

SIMPLE QUESTIONS

1. The text says Rowan 'darted' along the path.
2. She feels like she has come home. / She recognises the trees around her / including the tree she is named after.
3. She notices the bushes and trees have been burnt.
4. She knows there shouldn't be animals big enough to cause the damage.
5. She doesn't understand what could cause the heat. / She feels someone might need help.
6. It is emerald green. / It is far too big to belong to a bird.
7. She thinks it could be a creature in distress and wants to help.
8. It tries to flap its wings.
9. The dragon lets Rowan cuddle it. / It closes its eyes when she strokes it.
10. She hides behind a tree. / She carefully watches them through the leaves.

SENTENCE INFERENCE

1. They are tall.
2. protective
3. It's mysterious / dangerous / contains unknown things.
4. threatened
5. She went back the way she came.

THIS SUGGESTS...

1. Rowan feels connected to the forest.
2. There was a fire or something burned the trees.
3. It is unusual and could belong to a magical creature.
4. They have been hunting something.

EVIDENCE – TWO MARKS

1. She calls it beautiful. // She feels she has come home. // She recognises different trees. // She sees the tree she is named after.
2. She picks it up. // She cuddles it close to her chest. // She strokes it. // She whispers to it gently. // She promises to take it to her Grandpa for help // She tries to find its mum.
3. They are carrying weapons like spears, bows and arrows. // They are dragging a huge net, which suggests they are hunting something.
4. The eggshell is emerald green, a colour not typical for birds. // It is too large to belong to any bird Rowan has seen.

EVIDENCE – THREE MARKS

1. She steps behind an oak tree to stay hidden. / She peers carefully through the leaves. / She observes their weapons, like spears and bows. // She does not talk to them.
2. **Loving**: She cuddles the dragon close to her chest and strokes its head gently. // **Protective / helpful**: She promises to find its mother and plans to ask her Grandpa to heal its wing.
3. **Brave/ curious**: She ventures alone into the Dark Forest, even though it's unfamiliar and dangerous. // **Determined**: She carefully retraces her steps and looks for signs of the dragon's mother despite the challenges. **Loving/ Caring**: as per 2.

SUMMARISE

1. The Dark Forest feels dangerous and threatening.
2. Rowan thinks the dragon is beautiful and needs her help.

SEQUENCE

3. 2, 4, 1, 3

PREDICTION

4. The baby dragon's mother.

8. THE JOURNEY OF RUBY THE RED BLOOD CELL

SIMPLE QUESTIONS

1. Ruby uses words like 'exciting' / 'adventure' / 'thrill'.
2. The journey feels fast and exciting, like a roller coaster.
3. She mentions enjoying the speed of the journey.
4. She exchanges carbon dioxide for oxygen.
5. It says Ruby 'mingled' with fellow cells.
6. Ruby feels a 'sense of purpose' wash over her. / Hearing the surrounding cells 'sigh with gratitude' when she delivers oxygen.
7. She is a small part of a big system.
8. Ruby rests in the heart before the next cycle.
9. It maintains the balance of life.
10. Ruby is excited about the journeys to come.

SENTENCE INFERENCE

1. quick / fast
2. pride
3. It isn't needed / wanted.
4. excitement
5. There will be lots – too many to count.

THIS SUGGESTS...

1. Ruby thinks she has a key role.
2. Ruby finds it exciting.
3. Oxygen is essential for Ruby's role.
4. The cells are thankful for Ruby's work.

EVIDENCE – TWO MARKS

1. Ruby describes her work as 'an adventure' and 'exciting'. // She mentions feeling 'the thrill of discovery' / she enjoys every day being a 'new experience'.
2. Ruby compares the heart's contraction to being on a 'roller coaster.' // She describes the moment as 'electric', showing her excitement. // She feels adrenaline.
3. Ruby acknowledges that 'each cell has its own important role.' // She describes seeing white blood cells and platelets, each with their own missions.
4. Ruby says that taking in oxygen felt like a 'refreshing deep breath'. // She describes feeling 'revitalised' and ready for the journey ahead.

EVIDENCE – THREE MARKS

1. Answers referring to: a 'roller coaster' with 'adrenaline rushing.' // 'thrill of discovery' every day. // Ruby describes being 'revitalised'
2. **Proud:** 'a vital part of this magnificent system' / reflects on the importance of her work. // **Important:** She notes that her journey is 'not just about me, but about every living cell that depended on my delivery.'
3. **Fast:** Ruby describes the journey through the arteries as 'racing' and feeling the 'pulse of life' around her. // **Exciting:** She mentions the speed and says she 'revels' in the journey, showing her excitement.

SUMMARISE

1. Ruby thinks her work is exciting and meaningful.
2. Ruby thinks the heart is powerful and thrilling.

SEQUENCE

3. 3, 2, 1, 4

PREDICTION

4. Ruby will continue delivering oxygen.

9. WHERE I LIVE

SIMPLE QUESTIONS

1. Because the narrator is very small (an ant).
2. They use words like 'cower' and 'frightening'.
3. Because the narrator sees it as enormous.
4. To help the reader imagine something really big.

SENTENCE INFERENCE

1. For the ant, their home is normal / it is not the only home like that.
2. Excitement

THIS SUGGESTS…

1. They feel overwhelmed.

EVIDENCE – TWO MARKS

1. They compare features of the home to large natural areas such as oceans, mountains and the sun. // They use lots of words that mean large, like 'enormous', 'vast', 'monumental', 'cavernous' and more.

EVIDENCE – THREE MARKS

1. **Small:** Compares their surroundings to enormous objects like an 'ocean' and a 'mountain.' // **Scared:** They say the cushions 'make me cower', that the hall feels 'cavernous', and their life is 'frightening.' // **Normal:** They describe it as 'conventional' and 'not unique' and a 'normal size'.

SUMMARY

1. The narrator is playful.

10. THE VOICE OF VESUVIUS

SIMPLE QUESTIONS

1. Vesuvius watches over them and feels their happiness.
2. Vesuvius feels a deep rumble and pressure building.
3. They are running, their eyes are wide with fear and they look for shelter.
4. The ash and darkness make it hard to see and they don't know where to go.

SENTENCE INFERENCE

1. Happy
2. Joy

THIS SUGGESTS…

1. Pompeii has been completely covered.

EVIDENCE – TWO MARKS

1. People are running in fear. // Faces are wide with terror.

EVIDENCE – THREE MARKS

2. **Uncomfortable:** 'pressure growing within' or 'faint rumble'. // **Worried:** 'shift beneath my surface' or 'shiver of unease'.

SUMMARY, SEQUENCE AND PREDICTION

1. Vesuvius feels a sense of pride in watching over Pompeii.

11. ISADORA MOON SLEEPOVER

SIMPLE QUESTIONS

1. They talked about having a midnight feast and telling ghost stories.
2. She said it wouldn't be fair to enter the cake in the competition because they cheated.
3. She thought it would help them stay awake and add excitement to the sleepover.
4. She said her biggest wish was for them to stay best friends forever and live next door to each other.

SENTENCE INFERENCE

1. Answers referring to guilt or cheating
2. fear

THIS SUGGESTS…

1. She feels guilty about using magic.

EVIDENCE – TWO MARKS

1. She giggles when suggesting they eat the rest of the sprinkles. / She whispers enthusiastically about staying awake.

EVIDENCE – THREE MARKS

2. **Honest:** Isadora admits that using magic for the cake was unfair and feels bad about it. // **Caring:** She thinks about how Oliver and Bruno worked hard on their dinosaur cake and doesn't want to hurt their feelings. // **Good friend / loyal:** with supporting evidence.

SUMMARY

1. Zoe wants to enter the cake, but Isadora feels bad about using magic.

12. WILD WEST

SIMPLE QUESTIONS

1. work hard to grow food and survive / towns could be dangerous.
2. Freedom to own land build farms, or start businesses.
3. Slept outside under the stars / travelled long distances with cattle.
4. They were known for robbing banks and trains.

SENTENCE INFERENCE

1. Tough / difficult / challenging
2. Opportunity

THIS SUGGESTS...
1. Wild West life wasn't suitable for everyone.

EVIDENCE – TWO MARKS
1. They are described as 'legendary' // She had 'amazing accuracy'.

EVIDENCE – THREE MARKS
2. **Tough:** Settlers faced dangerous outlaws, wild animals and harsh weather. // **Hardworking:** Families worked hard to grow food and survive in challenging conditions.

SUMMARY
3. A skilled and bold performer who impressed audiences.

13. MY FRIEND THE ALIEN

SIMPLE QUESTIONS
1. It was delicious and they hadn't eaten anything like it before.
2. They didn't want to draw attention or seem strange.
3. They think the human is 'suffering from love' and don't see why the dog is special.
4. They wanted to avoid being chased and stay safe.

SENTENCE INFERENCE
1. Supermarket shopping trolleys.
2. sweat

THIS SUGGESTS...
1. Maxx is not interested in the dog.

EVIDENCE – TWO MARKS
1. Maxx mentions the 'nasty gas' and 'stinky water' coming from humans. // Maxx describes the closeness of humans as unpleasant and uncomfortable.

EVIDENCE – THREE MARKS
2. **Confused:** Maxx says, 'Google says these guys have a gazillion different kinds of feelings,' showing they find the variety overwhelming. // **Disgusted:** Maxx describes love as 'yuckiest' and reacts with 'Ewww,' suggesting they are put off by the concept.

SUMMARY
1. Maxx feels abandoned and lonely.

14. THE JUNGLE PERSONIFIED

SIMPLE QUESTIONS
1. He has fists 'like thunder' / is 'full of quiet strength'.
2. He sits like 'a king upon his green throne.'
3. He is 'silent as breath,'
4. It mentions a 'delicate fortress' // 'ready to trap the careless wanderer.'

SENTENCE INFERENCE
1. snake
2. spider

THIS SUGGESTS...
1. He is strong and determined.

EVIDENCE – TWO MARKS
1. 'feathers flash like forgotten dreams.' // 'twirls in the canopy' and 'sweet and wild' voice.

EVIDENCE – THREE MARKS
2. **Powerful/strong:** 'Each footfall marks a memory in the soil.' **Ancient / old:** 'He wears his heavy crown of ivory and time.'

SUMMARY
1. The armoured knight is slow and heavy, while the winged dancer is light and quick.

15. MISCHIEF ON THE MOORS

SIMPLE QUESTIONS
1. The gate was broken and the fence was destroyed.
2. Mr. Butchart was on foot and they were still on bikes.
3. Moving made him sink deeper into the bog.
4. He looked at the bog, realised he might drown and immediately gave up the pixie.

SENTENCE INFERENCE
1. Cheeky / naughty / mischievous
2. Danger

THIS SUGGESTS...
1. She is worried about Mr. Butchart.

EVIDENCE – TWO MARKS
1. He is sinking further with every movement. / The bog is described as 'slurping' and 'sucking,' showing it is pulling him down.

EVIDENCE – THREE MARKS
2. They ride their bikes through dangerous terrain, including broken fences and muddy paths. // They cross the stepping stones in rapid jumps, showing no fear of falling. // They confront Mr. Butchart and help him escape from the bog, even though it's risky.

SUMMARY
1. Libby wants to save the pixie, but Mr. Butchart sees it as a way to get rich.

16. THE LAB BOOK OF MARIE CURIE

SIMPLE QUESTIONS
1. Marie Curie says she is 'buzzing with excitement' in her lab.
2. She says she is 'cherishing the moments' together in the lab.
3. Marie Curie reminds herself to be careful.
4. Marie Curie says she feels 'lost without him' and is writing 'through tears'.

SENTENCE INFERENCE
1. Because Pierre is not there to share it with
2. Danger

THIS SUGGESTS...
1. It is unusual and fascinating.

EVIDENCE – TWO MARKS
1. She says she is 'buzzing with excitement.' // She says: 'I can hardly believe it,'

EVIDENCE – THREE MARKS
2. **Determined:** she continues her work even after the death of her husband Pierre. // **Brave:** she handles dangerous materials, enduring burns and other risks.

SUMMARY
1. A dedicated and passionate scientist who perseveres despite challenges.

17. MARK OF THE CYCLOPS

SIMPLE QUESTIONS
1. He lists all the exciting and dangerous events they experienced.
2. The roads are smelly, the people are loud and the harbour is full of activity.
3. They sneaked into the bathroom to wash and use the perfumed oil.
4. He hopes it will inspire him to write admired poems.

SENTENCE INFERENCE
1. Old
2. palace

THIS SUGGESTS...
1. He is wealthy and enjoys hosting.

EVIDENCE – TWO MARKS
1. They gave themselves a long wash and used the perfumed oil. // They didn't want their masters to know they appreciated the luxuries.

EVIDENCE – THREE MARKS
2. **Lively / Busy:** The text describes Corinth as having noisy streets and a reputation as the liveliest capital. **Beautiful:** The description of the temple, mosaics and sacred spring shows it's a striking place.

SUMMARY
1. He finds it beautiful and impressive.

18. THE BOY WHO GREW A TREE

SIMPLE QUESTIONS
1. The library had been closed and unused for a while.
2. Its leaves drooped and the trunk looked like it was leaning and tired.
3. He wanted the tree to get more sunlight to help it grow.
4. It had grown a full metre and looked healthy again.

SENTENCE INFERENCE
1. They were heavy
2. pride

THIS SUGGESTS...
1. The tree is struggling to survive.

EVIDENCE – TWO MARKS
1. It grew a full metre overnight, which isn't normal for a tree. // Timi feels it looks healthier after just a little sunlight and water.
2. He checks if the floorboards are damp to ensure the tree has had enough water. // He promises himself to come back the next day to check on it again.

SUMMARY
1. Timi sees the library as a magical and special place.

19. PING AND THE MISSING RING

SIMPLE QUESTIONS
1. Because she is packing her suitcase and can barely contain her energy.
2. She feels like she has bubbles and springs inside her that are hard to control.
3. Her mother already placed Ping's clothes in a pile for her to pack.
4. She gets excited about noticing clues like the hair and sock to figure out who used the suitcase.

SENTENCE INFERENCE
1. Ping is so excited she can't stay still.
2. caring

THIS SUGGESTS...
1. She is graceful and elegant.

EVIDENCE – TWO MARKS
1. She tries to keep a 'lid' on her excitement but often bursts out unexpectedly'. // She feels like she has 'bubbles in her body' that make her want to giggle and roar.

EVIDENCE – THREE MARKS
2. **Admires:** Ping describes her mother's movements as 'graceful' and 'like a dance,' showing she looks up to her. // **Loves:** Ping notices small, tender details, like how her mother washes apples 'as though she were bathing a newborn baby.'

SUMMARY
1. Ping admires her mother's grace and calmness.

20. ROAD TRIP USA

SIMPLE QUESTIONS
1. Route has unique sights like classic diners and neon signs that make it memorable for travellers.
2. Places like mountains, deserts, cities and towns, showing a lot of variety.
3. It mentions 'must-see' destinations, which means lots of people want to visit them.
4. Unusual things like the 'Old Faithful Geyser' and wildlife, which are unique to Yellowstone.

SENTENCE INFERENCE
1. That the cities are full of energy / life and things to do.
2. awe

THIS SUGGESTS...
1. It is vast and impressive.

EVIDENCE – TWO MARKS
1. The view stretches for miles // The rocks glow red and orange in the sunlight.

EVIDENCE – THREE MARKS
2. **Nostalgic or historic:** The text mentions 'classic roadside diners, quirky motels and neon signs' // **Unique or interesting:** It has 'giant statues and unusual roadside attractions like the Cadillac Ranch' and 'the world's largest rocking chair'.

SUMMARY
3. They enjoy the unique and historic sights along the way.

ACKNOWLEDGEMENTS

The authors and publisher gratefully acknowledge the permission granted to reproduce the copyright material in this book.

PAGES 8–9
Bella's Den by Berlie Doherty © Berlie Doherty, 1997, published by Barrington Stoke. Reproduced by kind permission by David Higham Associates. Text copyright.

PAGES 28–29
The Great (Food) Bank Heist by Onjali Q. Raúf. Reprinted by permission of HarperCollins Publishers Ltd © 2021, Onjali Q. Raúf.

PAGE 48
Ava's Gone from *Who Let the Words Out?* © Joshua Seigal 2023. Reproduced with the permission of Bloomsbury Publishing Plc.

PAGE 49
Pets in Class from *Who Let the Words Out?* © Joshua Seigal 2023. Reproduced with the permission of Bloomsbury Publishing Plc.

PAGES 58–59
Kid Normal © Greg James and Chris Smith 2017. Reproduced with the permission of Bloomsbury Publishing Plc.

PAGES 68–69
Wildsmith: Into the Dark Forest © Liz Flanagan 2023. Reproduced with the permission of UCLan Publishing.

PAGES 88–89
Where I Live from *Who Let the Words Out?* © Joshua Seigal 2023. Reproduced with the permission of Bloomsbury Publishing Plc.

PAGES 96-97
Isadora Moon Has a Sleepover © Harriet Muncaster 2019. Reproduced with permission of Oxford Publishing Limited through PLSclear.

PAGES 104–105
My Friend the Alien © Zanib Mian 2020. Reproduced with the permission of Bloomsbury Publishing Plc.

PAGES 112–113
Mischief on the Moors © Stephen Davies 2023. Reproduced with the permission of Bloomsbury Publishing Plc

PAGES 120–121
Mark of the Cyclops: An Ancient Greek Mystery © Saviour Pirotta 2017. Reproduced with the permission of Bloomsbury Publishing Plc.

PAGES 124–125
The Boy Who Grew a Tree © Polly Ho-Yen 2022. Reproduced with the permission of Knights Of Publishing.

PAGES 128–129
Ping and the Missing Ring © Emma Shevah 2021. Reproduced with the permission of Bloomsbury Publishing Plc.

Every effort has been made to trace copyright holders and to obtain their permission for the use of copyright material. The publisher apologizes for any errors or omissions in the above list and would be grateful if notified of any corrections that should be incorporated in future reprints or editions of this book.